Workshop on Computational Modeling of Polysynthetic Languages 2018

Santa Fe, New Mexico, USA
25 August 2018

ISBN: 978-1-5108-6917-2

COLING 2018

The 27th International Conference
on Computational Linguistics

Proceedings of the Workshop on
Computational Modeling of Polysynthetic Languages

Saturday, August 25, 2018
Santa Fe, New Mexico, USA

Introduction

The workshop on Computational Modeling of Polysynthetic Languages addresses the needs for documentation, archiving, creation of corpora and teaching materials that are specific to polysynthetic languages. Documentation and corpus-building challenges arise for many languages, but the complex morphological makeup of polysynthetic languages makes consistent documentation particularly difficult. This workshop is the first ever meeting where researchers and practitioners working on polysynthetic languages discuss common problems and difficulties, and it is intended as the capstone to establishing possible collaborations and ongoing partnerships of the relevant issues. One of our intentions is to discuss the possibility of creating a shared task in order to increase opportunities to share challenges and solutions.

One of the goals of the workshop is to create dialog between those language professionals who collect and annotate language data for polysynthetic languages, those who are committed to linguistic analysis, those who develop and apply computational methods to these languages, and those who are dedicated to revitalization through policy, education and community activism. Too often, these communities do not interact enough to benefit each other, so there is a lost opportunity cost all around. This lost opportunity, especially in the case of endangered languages, is one that cannot be recuperated. Thus, it is urgent to work towards the goal of leveraging each other's efforts.

On a lighter note, the Workshop has had an informal pre-title "All Together Now" to reflect the linguistic and typological nature of polysynthesis.

Organizers

Workshop Chair:

Judith L. Klavans, Senior Scientist, Army Research Laboratory and University of Maryland
Ph.D. Linguistics. University College, University of London, England
Judith.l.klavans.civ@mail.mil judith.klavans@gmail.com

Organizing Committee:

Anna Kazantseva, Research Officer - National Research Council of Canada
Ph.D. Computer Science, University of Ottawa
Anna.Kazantseva@nrc-cnrc.gc.ca

Roland Kuhn, Senior Research Officer at National Research Council of Canada
Ph.D. Computer Science, McGill University
Roland.Kuhn@cnrc-nrc.gc.ca

Steve LaRocca, Team Lead, Multilingual Computing, Army Research Laboratory
Ph.D. Linguistics, Georgetown University
stephen.a.larocca.civ@mail.mil

Jeffrey Micher, Researcher, Multilingual Computing, Army Research Laboratory
M.A. Linguistics, University of Pittsburgh,
M.S. Language Technologies Carnegie Mellon University
jeffrey.c.micher.civ@mail.mil

Clare Voss, Team Lead, Multilingual Computing, Army Research Laboratory
Ph.D. Computer Science, University of Maryland
clare.r.voss.civ@mail.mil

Consulting Co-organizers:

Maria Polinsky, Professor and Associate Director of the Language Science Center, University of Maryland. Ph.D. Linguistics, Institute for Linguistics of the Russian Academy of Sciences, Moscow.
polinsky@umd.edu

Omer Preminger, Associate Professor of Linguistics, University of Maryland. Ph.D. Linguistics, The Massachusetts Institute of Technology.
omerp@umd.edu

Program Committee:

Since the goal of this workshop has been to explore practical applications of recent developments in linguistics and computational linguistics to the preservation and revitalization of North American indigenous languages, and to build on the long history of research on polysynthesis combined with the more current computational interest in processing morphologically complex languages, the Program Committee consists of theoretical linguists, computational linguists, anthropological linguists, experts in language revitalization. Thus we have established a valuable balance in expertise.

Antti Arppe, University of Alberta
Mark Baker, Rutgers University
Steven Bird, Charles Darwin University
Aaron Broadwell, University of Florida
Lauren Clemens, State University of New York - Albany
Christopher Cox, Carleton University
Amy Dahlstrom, University of Chicago
Henry Davis, University of British Columbia
Jeff Good, State University of New York - Buffalo
Jeremy Green, Six Nations Polytechnic
David Harrison, Swarthmore College
Gary Holton, University of Hawaii - Mānoa
Marianne Ignace, Simon Fraser University
Judith Klavans, Army Research Laboratory
Roland Kuhn, National Research Council of Canada
Stephen LaRocca, Army Research Laboratory
Lori Levin, Carnegie Mellon University, National Research Council of Canada
Gina-Anne Levow, University Washington
Patrick Littell, Carnegie Mellon University
Alexa Little, 7000 Languages project
Jordan Lachler, University of Alberta
Mitch Marcus, University of Pennsylvania
Michael Maxwell, Center for Advanced Study of Language, University of Maryland
Jeffrey Micher, Army Research Laboratory
Marianne Mithun, University California - Santa Barbara
Timothy Montler, University of North Texas
Rachel Nordlinger, University of Melbourne
Boyan Onyshkevich, US Government
Carl Rubino – US Government
Lane Schwartz, University Illinois - Urbana-Champaign
Richard Sproat, Google Research
Clare Voss, Army Research Laboratory
Michelle Yuan, Massachusetts Institute of Technology

Invited Speaker: Brian Maracle (Owennatekha), Kanyen'kéha (Mohawk) First Nation[1]

Brian Maracle, also known as, author, journalist and radio host (born in 1947 in Detroit, Michigan). Brian Maracle is a member of the Mohawk First Nation and a passionate advocate for the preservation of the Kanyen'kehaka (Mohawk) language.

Brian Maracle was raised on the Six Nations Grand River Territory Reserve in Ohsweken, Ontario, until he was five when his family moved to the state of New York. He earned a BA from Dartmouth College in 1969 before going to work for Indigenous organizations in Vancouver during the 1970s. In 1980 he relocated to Ottawa to study journalism at Carleton University, graduating in 1982. Maracle was a journalist in the 1980s, writing for the *Globe and Mail* and covering Indigenous issues for mainstream and Indigenous media. He also hosted the CBC Radio program *Our Native Land*, which began in 1965 and ran for 21 years, the first national radio program focused on Indigenous culture and issues.

In 1993, Maracle's first book, *Crazywater: Native Voices on Addiction and Recovery*, was published. The book is the compilation of 200 interviews, channelling traditional oral history, conducted across the country by Maracle during three years of research. The interview subjects are exemplified by the book's 75 people who represent a cross-section of society. The importance of the book is in the voice it gives to the Indigenous perspective on alcohol and drugs, which comes long after the dominant white culture—academics, social scientists, government authorities and medical experts—has expounded on the issue.

After the book came out, Maracle left Ottawa and moved back to his reserve. His experiences in returning led Maracle to write *Back on the Rez, finding the way home* which was published in 1996. He recounts the struggles of an urban dweller assimilating to life in the country while he struggles with understanding the Mohawk language. He points out how the dominant white culture has played a significant role in destroying Indigenous identity and culture, but notes also the flaws in Indigenous society and how the community is torn between white culture and tradition.

After Maracle moved back to his reserve, he began to learn the Mohawk language and, with his wife Audrey, established a full-time adult immersion language school, Onkwawenna Kentyohkwa, in 1998. Maracle eventually all but abandoned his writing career to devote himself to revitalizing the Mohawk language, employing his skills to host a radio program called *Tewatonhwehsen!* (Let's have a good time!) and writing a blog in Mohawk. In 2012, Maracle's new media collaboration with his daughter Zoe Leigh Hopkins was presented at the 13th Annual imagineNATIVE Film and Media Arts Festival. Their sound art piece, *Karenniyohston – Old Songs Made Good*, blends oral language and sound art in a 30-minute adaptation of five national and cultural anthems from Canada, the UK and the US.

---

[1] Taken from https://www.thecanadianencyclopedia.ca/en/article/brian-maracle/, author Laura Nielson Bonikowdsky (2013), Revised by Michele Felice (2017)

Panel: "Revitalization: Bridging Technology and Language Education"

The purpose of this panel is to address and debate some of the controversial issues that arise in the process of establishing better communication and building a way to bridge the research and applications gaps between and among researchers and practitioners. Some of these issues include such provocative and often divisive points.

Invited Panel Speakers

Inée Yang Slaughter, Executive Director, Indigenous Language Institute

Inée Slaughter has been with the Indigenous Language Institute since 1995. ILI was founded as the Institute for the Preservation of the Original Languages of the Americas (IPOLA) by Joanna Hess in 1992. In 1997, IPOLA extended its scope and in 2000, IPOLA was changed to Indigenous Language Institute (ILI) to reflect working relations with all indigenous communities, nationally and internationally. ILI provides the tools and training to help First Nation language teachers and learners help themselves in their efforts to bring language back into everyday lives of the People. ILI runs local and national workshops and teacher training sessions as well as the annual Indigenous Language Institute Symposium (ILIS) in New Mexico that invites presenters to address topics for language practitioners. Inée is of Korean heritage, born and raised in Japan, and is fluent in Japanese, Korean, and English.

Zoe Leigh Hopkins, Independent Filmaker and Director, Educator, Activist

Zoe Hopkins grew up in a Heiltsuk fishing village on the coast of British Columbia, home to her mother and maternal family, in the heart of the Great Bear Rainforest. She is an alumna of the Sundance Institute's Feature Film Program and her short films have premiered at the Sundance Film Festival and the Worldwide Short Film Festival. Her 2013 short, *Mohawk Midnight Runners* was named Best Canadian Short Drama at the 2013 imagineNATIVE Film + Media Arts Festival in Toronto, Ontario. In 2017, her feature film *Kayak to Klemtu* won the Air Canada Audience Choice Award. She now lives in her father's community of Six Nations, where she teaches the Mohawk language online to students across Turtle Island (North America). (from http://www.northernstars.ca/zoe-hopkins/)

Lori Levin, Research Professor, Language Technologies Institute, Carnegie Mellon University

Lori Levin holds a B.A. Linguistics, University of Pennsylvania, 1979 and a Ph.D. Linguistics, MIT, 1986. Her research interests range from theoretical to computational linguistics. In the language documentation area, she was funded by the Chilean Ministry of Education under the Language Technologies Institute's AVENUE project to collect data and produce language technologies that support bilingual education. The main resource that came out of this partnership is a Mapudungun-Spanish parallel corpus consisting of approximately 200,000 words of text and 120 hours of transcribed speech. In the education domain, Lori has been a leader and organizer of the North American Computational Linguistics Olympiad (NACLO), a contest in which high-school students solve linguistic puzzles thereby learning about the diversity and consistency of language.

Table of Contents

This page intentionally left blank.

Conference Program

Computational Modeling of Polysynthetic Languages

Judith L. Klavans, Ph.D.
US Army Research Laboratory
2800 Powder Mill Road
Adelphi, Maryland 20783
Judith.l.klavans.civ@mail.mil
Judith.klavans@gmail.com

Abstract

Given advances in computational linguistic analysis of complex languages using Machine Learning as well as standard Finite State Transducers, coupled with recent efforts in language revitalization, the time was right to organize a first workshop to bring together experts in language technology and linguists on the one hand with language practitioners and revitalization experts on the other. This one-day meeting provides a promising forum to discuss new research on polysynthetic languages in combination with the needs of linguistic communities where such languages are written and spoken. Finally, this overview article summarizes the papers to be presented, along with goals and purpose.

Motivation

Polysynthetic languages are characterized by words that are composed of multiple morphemes, often to the extent that one long word can express the meaning contained in a multi-word sentence in language like English. To illustrate, consider the following example from Inuktitut, one of the official languages of the Territory of Nunavut in Canada. The morpheme -*tusaa*- (shown in boldface below) is the root, and all the other morphemes are synthetically combined with it in one unit.[1]

(1) **tusaa**-tsia-runna-nngit-tu-alu-u-junga
    hear-well-be.able-NEG-DOER-very-BE-PART.1.S
    'I can't hear very well.'

Kabardian (Circassian), from the Northwest Caucasus, also shows this phenomenon, with the root -*še*- shown in boldface below:

(2) wə-q'ə-d-ej-z-ɣe-**še**-ž'e-f-a-te-q'əm
    2SG.OBJ-DIR-LOC-3SG.OBJ-1SG.SUBJ-CAUS-**lead**-COMPL-POTENTIAL-PAST-PRF-NEG
    'I would not let you bring him right back here.'

Polysynthetic languages are spoken all over the globe and are richly represented among Native North and South American families. Many polysynthetic languages are among the world's most endangered languages,[2] with fragmented dialects and communities struggling to preserve their linguistic heritage. In particular, polysynthetic languages can be found in the US Southwest (Southern Tiwa, Kiowa Tanoan family), Canada, Mexico (Nahuatl, Uto-Aztecan family), and Central Chile (Mapudungun,

---

[1] Abbreviations follow the Leipzig Glossing Rules; additional glosses are spelled out in full.
[2] In fact, the majority of the languages spoken in the world today are endangered and disappearing fast (See Bird, 2009). Estimates are that, of the approximately 7000 languages in the world today, at least one disappears every day (https://www.ethnologue.com).

1

Proceedings of Workshop on Polysynthetic Languages, pages 1–11
Santa Fe, New Mexico, USA, August 20-26, 2018.

Araucanian), as well as in Australia (Nunggubuyu, Macro-Gunwinyguan family), Northeastern Siberia (Chukchi and Koryak, both from the Chukotko-Kamchatkan family), and India (Sora, Munda family), as shown in the map below (Figure 1).

This workshop addresses the needs for documentation, archiving, creation of corpora and teaching materials that are specific to polysynthetic languages. Documentation and corpus-building challenges arise for many languages, but the complex morphological makeup of polysynthetic languages makes consistent documentation particularly difficult. This workshop is the first ever meeting where researchers and practitioners working on polysynthetic languages discuss common problems and difficulties, and it is intended as the capstone to establishing possible collaborations and ongoing partnerships of the relevant issues.

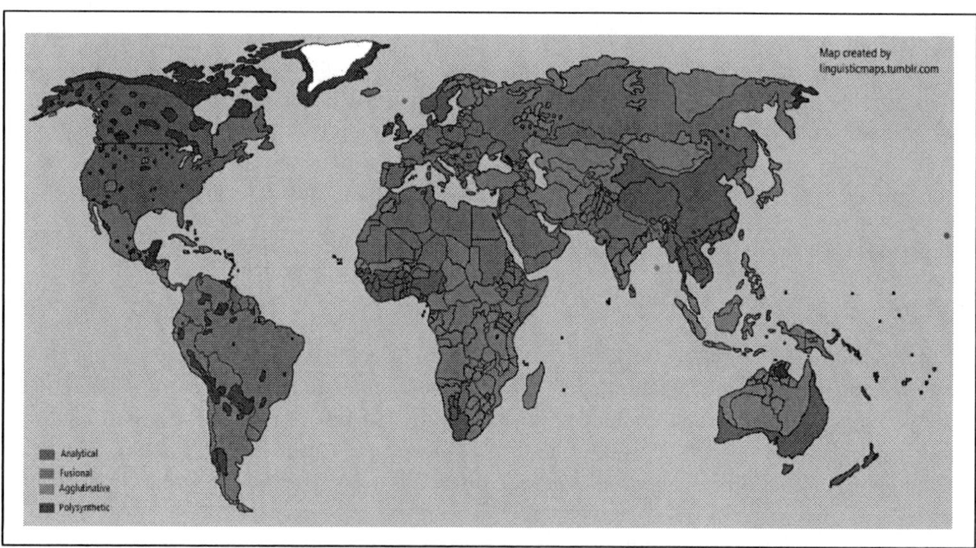

Figure 1: Polysynthetic Languages[3]

Defining Polysynthesis: An Ongoing Linguistic Challenge

Although there are many definitions of polysynthesis, there is often confusion on what constitutes the exact criteria and phenomena (Mithun 2017). Even authoritative sources categorize languages in conflicting ways.[4] Typically, polysynthetic languages demonstrate holophrasis, i.e. the ability of an entire sentence to be expressed in what is considered by native speakers to be just one word (Bird 2009). In

---

[3] http://linguisticmaps.tumblr.com/post/120857875008/513-morphological-typology-tonal-languages

[4] For example, the article in the *Oxford Research Encyclopedia of Linguistics* on "Polysynthesis: A Diachronic and Typological Perspective" by Michael Fortescue (Fortescue, 2016), a well-known expert on polysynthesis, lists Aymara as possibly polysynthetic, whereas others designate it as agglutinative (http://www.native-languages.org).

linguistic typology, the opposite of polysynthesis is isolation. Polysynthesis technically (etymological-ly) refers to how many morphemes there are per word. Using that criterion, the typological cline can be represented as follows:

(3) isolating/analytic languages > synthetic languages > polysynthetic languages

Adding another dimension of morphological categorization, languages can be distinguished by the degree of clarity of morpheme boundaries. If we apply this criterion, languages can be categorized according to the following typological cline:

(4) agglutinating > mildly fusional > fusional

Thus, a language might be characterized overall as polysynthetic and agglutinating, that is, generally a high number of morphemes per word, with clear boundaries between morphemes and thus easily segmentable. Another language might be characterized as polysynthetic and fusional, so again, many morphemes per word, but so many phonological and other processes have occurred that segmenting morphemes becomes less trivial.

So far we have discussed the morphological aspects of polysynthesis. Polysynthesis also has a number of syntactic ramifications, richly explored in the work of Baker (Baker 1997; 2002). He proposes a cluster of correlated syntactic properties associated with polysynthesis. Here we will mention just two of these properties: rich agreement (with the subject, direct object, indirect object, and applied objects if present) and omission of free-standing arguments (pro-drop).

Polysynthetic languages are of interest for both theoretical and practical reasons. On the theoretical side, these languages offer a potentially unique window into human cognition and language capabilities as well as into language acquisition (Mithun 1989; Greenberg 1960; Comrie 1981; Fortescue et al. 2017). They also pose unique challenges for traditional computational systems (Byrd et al. 1986). Even in allegedly cross-linguistic or typological analyses of specific phenomena, e.g. in forming a theory of clitics and cliticization (Klavans 1995), finding the full range of language types on which to test hypotheses proves difficult. Often, the data is simply not available so claims cannot be either refuted or supported fully.

On the applied side, many morphologically complex languages are crucial to purposes in domains ranging from health care,[5] search and rescue, to the maintenance of cultural history. Add to this the interest in low-resource languages (from Inuktitut and Yup'ik in the North and East of Canada with over 35,000 speakers, and all the way to Northwest Caucasian), which is important for linguistic, cultural and governmental reasons. Many of the data collections in these languages, when annotated and aligned well, can serve as input to systems to automatically create correspondences, and these in turn can be useful to teachers in creating resources for their learners (Adams, Neubig, Cohn, & Bird 2015). These languages are generally not of immediate commercial value, and yet the research community needs to cope with fundamental issues of language complexity. Consequently, research on these language could have unanticipated benefits on many levels.

---

[5] For example, the USAID has funded a program in the mountains of Ecuador to provide maternal care in Quechua-dominant areas to reduce maternal and infant mortality rates, taking into account local cultural and language needs (https://www.usaidassist.org). Quechua is highly agglutinative, not polysynthetic; it is spoken by millions of speakers and has few corpora with limited annotation.

Finally, many of these understudied languages occur in areas that are key for health concerns (e.g. the AIDS epidemic) and international security. Consider the map in Figure 2, which shows languages identified as Language Hotspots, i.e. low resource and/or endangered. For example, many languages in the Siberian peninsula (which is of strategic political importance) are endangered and polysynthetic. Comparing the two maps in Figures 1 and 2 shows these languages are more widespread than is commonly believed. Understanding theoretical mechanisms underlying the range of language types contributes to teaching, learning, maintaining and data-mining across both speech and text in these languages and beyond.

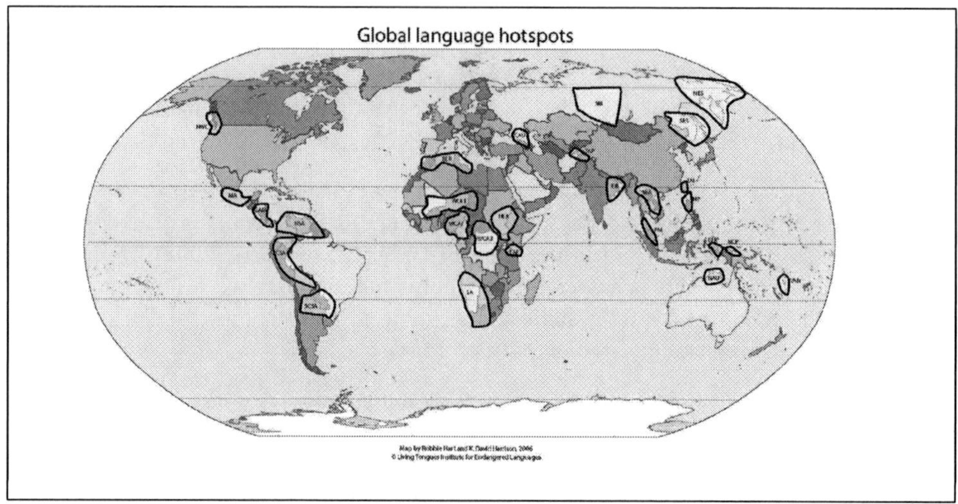

<u>Figure 2: Language Hotspots</u>[6]

Corpus Collection and Annotation

The more language data that is gathered and accurately analyzed, the more deep cross-linguistic analyses can be conducted which in turn will contribute to a range of fields including linguistic theory, language teaching and lexicography. For example, in examining cross-linguistic analyses of headedness, Polinsky (Polinsky 2012) gathered as much data as possible to examine the question of whether the noun-verb ratio differs across headedness types. She collected as much numerical data as she could identify across a sample of languages. However, she notes that:

"[T]he seemingly simple question of counting nouns and verbs is a quite difficult one; even obtaining data about the overall number of nouns and verbs proves to be an immense challenge. The ultimate consequence is that linguists lack reasonable tools to compare languages with respect to their lexical category size. Co-operation between theoreticians and lexicographers is of critical importance: just as comparative syntax received a big boost from the micro-comparative work on closely related languages (Romance; Germanic;

---

[6] https://www.swarthmore.edu/SocSci/langhotspots/resources/Hotspots%20Aug%202006%20copy.jpg

Semitic), so micro-comparative WordNet building may lead to important breakthroughs that will benefit the field as a whole." (Polinsky, 2012, *p. 351*)

One of the underlying causes of this difficulty is that there are many languages for which a clear lexical division between nouns and verbs has been challenged; these languages are characterized by a large class of roots that are used either nominally or verbally, and many of these languages typically have polysynthetic features (cf. Lois & Vapnarsky 2006 for Amerindian, Aranovich 2013 for Austronesian, Testelets et al. 2009 for Adyghe, Davis & Matthewson 2009, Watanabe 2017 for Salish). Without a clear definition of what counts as a verb and what as a noun, there is no reliable way to compute significant correlations. Thus, a deeper understanding of polysynthetic phenomena may well contribute to a more nuanced understanding of cross-language comparisons and generalizations and enable researchers to pose meaningful and answerable questions about comparative features across languages.

One of the goals of the workshop is to identify and build new resources, with annotation that is effective for a range of efforts, as outlined in Levow et al. (2017). We will ensure that all materials resulting from this workshop are listed in the LDC catalog with adequate metadata giving descriptions, pointers, terms and conditions and other facts necessary for use. What we have found is that there are corpora in many different places by different types of community actors, and often they are difficult to locate and obtain. Building models and theoretical descriptions can be challenging without adequate data, and this is a gap we plan to address along with the many others involved in this endeavor.

While collections of annotated corpora (spoken and written) for major isolating, agglutinative and inflectional languages exist (https://www.ldc.upenn.edu), there are significant additional complexities involved when it comes to polysynthetic languages, including:

- tokenization - what are the boundaries for units of meaning? How are morphology and syntax delimited?
- lemmatization - where is the root? which morphemes are affixes? which are clitics?
- part-of-speech tagging
- glossing and translation into other languages

Linguistic data in these languages, be it text or audio, is scarce. This has created challenges for language analysis as well as for revitalization efforts. Only recently have researchers started collecting well-designed corpora for polysynthetic languages, e.g. for Circassian (Arkhangelskiy & Lander 2016) or Arapaho (Kazeminejad et al. 2017).

Towards a shared task

Concomitant with the collection and cataloging of corpora, as part of the workshop, we aim to formulate a shared task, that meets the goals outlined in Levow, et al. (2017), namely, to "align the interests of the speech and language processing communities with those of endangered language documentation communities." Levow et al. 2017 propose an initial set of possible shared tasks based on the design principles of realism, typological diversity, accessibility of the shared task, accessibility of the resulting software, extensibility and nuanced evaluation. In addition to coordinating with the NSF-funded EL-STEC project, we have consulted with the SIGMORPHON organizers,[7] and Morpho Challenge project. We have also collaborated with organizers of the Documenting Endangered Languages Workshops (notably Jeff Good of the University at Buffalo). We have also coordinated with the NSF-funded CoLang program (Institute on Collaborative Language Research) at the University of Florida (http://colang.lin.ufl.edu/). Given the challenges of compiling a shared task, we have planned sessions during the workshop for participants to engage together in the creation of a shared task. In this way, we will involve community activists in the task formulation, which will lead to a higher chance of actually meeting local language needs.

Related Projects and Conferences

In recent years, there has been a surge of major research on many of these languages. For example, the first Endangered Languages (ELs) Workshop held in conjunction with ACL was held in 2014 and the second in 2017.[8] The National Science Foundation and the National Endowment for the Humanities jointly fund a program for research on ELs.[9] The US government through IARPA and DARPA both have programs for translation, including for low resource languages.[10] The IARPA BABEL project focused on keyword search over speech for a variety of typologically different languages, including some with polysynthetic features.

To reiterate, an interdisciplinary workshop specifically on the challenges of dealing with polysynthesis in computational linguistics has not been held before. The languages involved in Morph-Challenge (http://morpho.aalto.fi/events/morphochallenge/) did not include polysynthetic languages, nor did SIGMORPHON (http://ryancotterell.github.io/sigmorphon2016/). Given recent advances in computational morphology, a workshop that addresses the full range of morpho-syntactic features of language, extending to and including polysynthesis, is timely.

As indicated above, this workshop brings together researchers from multidisciplinary fields to address ongoing challenges and to compare outputs of various recent approaches, resulting in a lively venue for discussion and argument. The specific goals of the proposed workshop include:

1. To bring together experts in linguistic theory and computational linguistics with those working on preserving and reviving indigenous languages.

2. To discuss the potential of technologies (e.g., text-to-speech systems, segmentation of speech files by speaker, audio-indexing, morphological analysis) to assist in language revitalization.

3. To construct and annotate data sets in these languages for use by the relevant linguistic communities; these datasets can be used for research and practical applications.

---

[7] https://sites.google.com/view/conll-sigmorphon2017/home?authuser=0;
http://www.aclweb.org/old_anthology/W/W16/W16-20.pdf#page=22.

[8] http://www.acsu.buffalo.edu/~jcgood/ComputEL.html; http://altlab.artsrn.ualberta.ca/computel-2/.

[9] https://www.nsf.gov/funding/pgm_summ.jsp?pims_id=12816; https://www.neh.gov/grants/manage/general-information-neh-nsf-documenting-endangered-languages-fellowships.

[10] MATERIAL, https://www.iarpa.gov/index.php/research-programs/material and LORELEI,
http://www.darpa.mil/program/low-resource-languages-for-emergent-incidents, respectively.

4. To explore a deeper understanding of polysynthesis as a linguistic phenomenon.

Discussion of Workshop Papers

Eight papers were accepted to the Workshop. The languages and technologies discussed are wide-ranging and reflected the intended nature of the meeting as inclusive and exploratory. Languages include:

- Hinóno'eitíít - Arapaho (in English:), one of the highly-endangered Plains Algonquian languages (unknown numbers, ranging from 500 to 2500 speakers)

- Nahuatl, Wixarika and Yorem Nokki - from the Uto-Aztecan language family (estimated 1.5 million speakers)

- Kwak'wala - spoken by the Kwakwaka'wakw people (which means "those who speak Kwak'wala") and highly-endangered, belonging to the Wakashan language family (estimated 250 speakers).

- Kanyen'kéha (Ohsweken dialect) - language of the Iroquoian family commonly known as Mohawk, spoken in parts of Canada (Ontario and Quebec) and the United States (New York state) with about 3500 native speakers.

- Inuktitut - one of the principal Inuit languages used in parts of Newfoundland and Labrador, Quebec, the Northwest Territories and Nunavit, recognized as an official language in the Province of Nunavut with about 40,000 speakers.

- Chuckchi - a Chukotko–Kamchatkan language spoken in the easternmost extremity of Siberia, mainly in Chukotka Autonomous Okrug, rapidly decreasing in speakers with only about 500 native speakers left, down from nearly 8000 15 years ago.

We accepted one paper on an agglutinative language, with projected hypotheses on how the techniques might apply to some of the challenges of polysynthesis, namely;

- Lezgi (лезги), a statutory language of provincial identity in Dagestan Autonomous Republic west of the Caspian sea coast in the central Caucasus and a member of the Nakh-Daghestanian languages (approx. 600,000 speakers).

Our justification for including this paper is that we believe the authors may be able to test their techniques on other languages, so this paper will serve as a baseline for future research.

The technologies range from research on Finite State Transducers (FSTs), Statistical and Rule Based Machine Translation (SMTs), Conditional Random Fields (CRF) and CRF with Support Vector Machines (CRF-SVM), Neural Machine Translation (seq2seq) and Segmental Recurrent Neural Nets (SRNNs). Applications include morphological analysis, glossing, verb conjugation and generation, machine translation.

Although each article in the Workshop represents a specific and original contribution, either in method or in application of method to a given polysynthetic language or language group, as a whole, this collection of papers contributes to the literature that addresses the interdependence between linguistic theory, language revitalization, education and computational contributions. These relationships are reflected in the choice of invited speaker and in the panel.

Invited speaker

We are honored to have had the invited talk from Brian Maracle (Owennatekha, Turtle Clan, Mohawk), founder and teacher at the Onkwawenna Kentyohkwa Mohawk immersion school and head of the Mohawk-language school on the Six Nations Reserve near Brantford, Ontario. Maracle has been a language activist for nearly 25 years and has developed and published materials, as well as teaching adults and young people. He left a lucrative career to return to the reservation of his youth. His book <u>Back on the Rez: Finding the Way Home</u> (Penguin 1993) documents his path back and struggles to understand meetings held in the Kanyen'kehaka (Mohawk) language. These experiences led to his groundbreaking work in language revitalization.[11] Brian's dynamic and deep commitment to language documentation, teaching, and policy have had an impact on many people from linguists to anthropologists to teachers to elders to children and even to politicians.

Invited Panel – How Can We Work Together?

One of the goals of the Workshop is to create dialog between those language professionals who collect and annotate language data for polysynthetic languages, those who are committed to linguistic analysis, those who develop and apply computational methods to these languages, and those who are dedicated to revitalization through policy, education and community activism. Too often, these communities do not interact enough to benefit each other, so there is a lost opportunity cost all around. This lost opportunity, especially in the case of endangered languages, is one that cannot be recuperated. Thus, it is urgent to work towards the goal of leveraging each other's efforts.

Towards this end, we have organized a panel the purpose of which is to address and debate some of the controversial issues that arise in the process of establishing better communication. Some of these issues include such provocative and often divisive points such as:

- I am a teacher and none of your so-called useful tools are of any use to me. Why can't you come to my classroom and see what we really need?
- I am a computer scientist and I want to find out what is the best method to use to figure out how to morphologically analyze and label your really long words? How much text can you annotate for me so that I can train my systems?
- I am a speech recognition expert and I really need more data of spoken language transcribed into an accurate phonetic representation? Why can't you just ask people to make some recordings for me and then turn that into text?
- I am a revitalization expert and I want to establish new policy for my town so we can get a new school started. If you're a linguist, what can you tell me about other programs and how it might help in enforcing cultural identity and competence so I can convince people that we need funding?

---

[11] http://www.thecanadianencyclopedia.ca/en/article/brian-maracle/.

- I am developing curricula for a set of new classes for my endangered language. What kind of experience do you have in making dictionaries so my students can look up words they don't know?
- I am the child in a family where my parents and grandparents only speak their local language and not the dominant language of the government. I want to make sure that all important government documents are translated into my local language so the many elders like mine are empowered and so that I can pass this language onto my children. You are a computational linguist so how can you help? In fact, do you even care about this?

Future work will include follow up on documentation, corpus collection, revitalization, annotation, tools for analysis and methods to contribute both to the wide range of fields this research draws upon and impacts.

Acknowledgements:

Of the many workshops this author has organized and of the many program chairships she has held, she has never experienced 100% fulfillment of reviewing commitments from the program committee. The reviewers were thorough and detailed, which was deeply appreciated by the authors. More than one author thanked the organizing committee for the exhaustive in-depth anonymous reviews from the different perspectives of the fields represented. I believe this is due to the fact that each of the reviewers is committed to language maintenance, to linguistic accuracy and to the potential for computational approaches to make a contribution to teaching and learning of these rich and challenging languages.

We are especially grateful to the University of Maryland, especially Omer Preminger and Maria Polinsky for discussions on focus and purpose for the workshop; to the National Science Foundation for funding a Research Experience for Undergraduates (REU) proposal under an award to Maria Polinsky at the University of Maryland entitled "Cleaning, Organizing, and Uniting Linguistic Databases (the CLOUD Project)" [BCS 1619857] to support three undergraduates to attend the conference and to perform research on papers, authors and language revitalization efforts relevant to their undergraduate training; to Aaron Broadwell, who has headed the 2018 CoLang program and who was helpful in identifying promising undergraduates for the REU; to the COLING organizers, program committee and COLING Workshop organizers. The Army Research Laboratory in Adelphi, Maryland has supported three of the conference organizers and the National Research Council of Canada has supported two of the conference organizers in this endeavor.

Bibliography

Adams, O., Neubig,, G., Cohn, T., & Bird, S. (2015). Inducing bilingual lexicons from small quantities of sentence-aligned phonemic transcriptions. *Proceedings of the International Workshop on Spoken Language Translation (IWSLT 2015)*. Da Nang, Vietnam.

Aranovich, R. (2013). Transitivity and polysynthesis in Fijian. Language 89: 465-500.

Arkhangelskiy, T. A., & Lander, Y. A. (2016) Developing a polysynthetic language corpus: problems and solutions. *Computational Linguistics and Intellectual Technologies: Proceedings of the International Conference "Dialogue 2016"*, June 104, 2016.

Baker, M. C. (1996). *The polysynthesis parameter.* New York: Oxford University Press.

Baker, M.C. (2002). *Atoms of language.* New York: Basic Books.

Bird, S. (2009). Natural language processing and linguistic fieldwork . *Computational Linguistics, 35* (3), 469-474.

Byrd, R. J., Klavans, J. L., Aronoff, M., & Anshen, F. (1986). Computer methods for morphological analysis. *Proceedings of the 24th annual meeting on Association for Computational Linguistics* (pp. 120-127). Stroudsberg, PA: Association for Computational Linguistics.

Comrie, B. (1981). *Language Universals and Linguistic Typology.* Oxford: Blackwell.

Davis, H., & Mattewson, L. (2009). Issues in Salish syntax and semantics. *Language and Linguistics Compass 3,* 1097-1166.

Fortescue, M. (2016). Polysynthesis: A Diachronic and Typological Perspective . In M. Aronoff (ed.) *Oxford Encyclopedia of Linguistics.* Oxford, Oxford, England: Oxford University Press.

Fortescue, M. (1994). Polysynthetic morphology . (R. E. al., Ed.) *The encyclopedia of language and linguistic, 5,* 2600–2602.

Fortescue, M., Mithun, M., & Evans, N. (Eds.). (2017). *The Oxford Handbook of Polysynthesis.* Oxford: Oxford University Press.

Greenberg, J. H. (1960). A quantitative approach to the morphological typology of language . *International Journal of Linguistics,, 26,* 178–194.

Kazeminejad, G., Cowell , A., & Hulden , M. (2017). Creating lexical resources for polysynthetic languages—the case of Arapaho. *Proceedings of the 2nd Workshop on the Use of Computational Methods in the Study of Endangered Languages* (pp. 10-18). Honolulu: Association for Computational Linguistics.

Klavans, J. L. (1995). *On Clitics and Cliticization: The Interaction of Morphology, Phonology, and Syntax.* New York: Garland .

Levow, G.-A., Bender, E., Littell, P., Howell, K., Chelliah, S., Crowgey, J., et al. (2017). STREAMLInED Challenges: Aligning Research Interests with Shared Tasks. *Proceedings of ComputEL-2: 2nd Workshop on Computational Methods for Endangered Languages, .*

Lois, X., & Vapnarsky, V. (2006.). Root indeterminacy and polyvalence in Yukatecan Mayan languages. In X. Lois, & V. Vapnarsky (Eds.). *Lexical categories and root clauses in Amerindian languages* (pp. 69-115). Bern: Peter Lang.

Mithun, M. (1989). The acquisition of polysynthesis. *Journal of Child Language, 16,* 285–312.

Mithun, M. (2017). Argument marking in the polysynthetic verb and its implications. In M. Fortescue, M. Mithun, & N. Evans (Eds.), *The Oxford Handbook of Polysynthesis* (pp. 30-58). Oxford, UK: Oxford University Press.

Polinsky, M. (2012). Headedness, again. *UCLA Working Papers in Linguistics, Theories of Everything. 17,* pp. 348-359. Los Angeles: UCLA.

Sadock, J. (1986.). Some Notes on Noun Incorporation. *Language , 62,,* 19–31.

Testelets Ya. (ed.). (2009). *Aspekty polisintetizma: Očerki po grammatike adygejskogo jazyka [Aspects of poly-synthesis: Essays on Adyghe grammar]*, (pp. 17-120). Moscow: Russian University for the Humanities.

Watanabe, H. (2017). The polysynthetic nature of Salish. In Fortescue, M., Mithun, M., & Evans, N. (Eds.). (2017). *The Oxford Handbook of Polysynthesis* (pp. 623-642). Oxford: Oxford University Press.

A Neural Morphological Analyzer for Arapaho Verbs Learned from a Finite State Transducer

Sarah Moeller and **Ghazaleh Kazeminejad** and **Andrew Cowell** and **Mans Hulden**
Department of Linguistics
University of Colorado
`first.last@colorado.edu`

Abstract

We experiment with training an encoder-decoder neural model for mimicking the behavior of an existing hand-written finite-state morphological grammar for Arapaho verbs, a polysynthetic language with a highly complex verbal inflection system. After adjusting for ambiguous parses, we find that the system is able to generalize to unseen forms with accuracies of 98.68% (unambiguous verbs) and 92.90% (all verbs).

1 Introduction

One of the clear successes in computational modeling of linguistic patterns has been that of finite state transducer (FST) models for morphological analysis and generation (Koskenniemi, 1983; Beesley and Karttunen, 2003; Hulden, 2009; Lindén et al., 2009). Given enough linguistic expertise and investment in developing such models, FSTs provide the capability to analyze any well-formed word in a language. Although FST models generally rely on lexicons, they can also be extended to handle complex inflected word forms outside the lexicon as long as morphophonological regularities are obeyed. Even ill-formed words can be mapped to a "closest plausible reading" through FST engineering (Beesley and Karttunen, 2003). On the downside, developing a robust FST model for a given language is very time-consuming and requires knowledge of both the language and finite-state modeling tools (Maxwell, 2015). Development of a finite-state grammar tends to follow a Pareto-style tradeoff where the bulk of the grammar can be developed very quickly, and the long tail of remaining effort tends to focus on lexicon expansion and difficult corner cases.

In this paper we describe an experiment in training a neural encoder-decoder model to replicate the behavior of an existing morphological analyzer for the Arapaho language (Kazeminejad et al., 2017). Our purpose is to evaluate the feasibility of bootstrapping a neural analyzer with a hand-developed FST grammar, particularly if we train from an incomplete selection of word forms in the hand-developed grammar. A successful morphological analyzer is essential for downstream applications, such as speech recognition and machine translation, that could provide Arapaho speakers access to common tools similar to Siri or Google Translate that might support and accelerate language revitalization efforts.

2 Background & Related Work

Neural network models for word inflection have increased in popularity, particularly following the two SIGMORPHON and CoNLL-SIGMORPHON shared tasks (Cotterell et al., 2016; Cotterell et al., 2017). Most of the work in this domain relies on training encoder-decoder models used in machine translation to perform 'translations' of base forms and grammatical specifications into output forms, such as `fly +V +3PPres` ↦ `flies`, or vice versa. While such models can produce very reliable systems with a few thousand examples, the small available sample of polysynthetic languages indicate they are slightly more difficult to learn. Compare, for example, the accuracies of the best teams at CoNLL-SIGMORPHON 2017 between Navajo (92.30%) and Quechua[1] (99.90%). A remarkable detail about the neural inflection

---

[1] An agglutinating language with complex morphology, though not considered polysynthetic.

Proceedings of Workshop on Polysynthetic Languages, pages 12–20
Santa Fe, New Mexico, USA, August 20-26, 2018.

models is that in the 2017 shared task they were found to generalize beyond feature combinations that they had witnessed. Thus, for example, if a system had seen future tense forms and plurals separately, but never seen the combination of the two, they could produce the combination quite reliably (Cotterell et al., 2017). This effect was most striking for Basque, which has a highly complex, albeit very regular, verb system. One of the main purposes of the experiments described in this paper is to capitalize on this capacity to automatically generalize beyond what has been explicitly encoded in an FST grammar.

Standard morphological analyzers tend to be designed to return all 'plausible' parses of a word. In English, for example, this means that in practice any verb (e.g. **sell**) would always be alternatively parsed as a noun reading as well; likewise for the third person present form, **sells**, which could be parsed as a plural noun. This adds complications to the design of a neural model intended to mimic the behavior of a classical morphological analyzer, since it needs to return multiple options, and a neural encoder-decoder really encapsulates a distribution over all possible output strings Σ^* for any input string read by the encoder. An unexpected "advantage" of applying this to polysynthetic languages is that, while the verb complex in polysynthetic languages tends to be very intricate and is time-consuming to model, it proffers typically less ambiguity of a parse (as will be discussed in Section 6). Even when ambiguous readings are possible, they tend to be highly systematic. Silfverberg and Hulden (2018) documents a neural model from an FST model for Finnish (an agglutinative language) to retrieve all plausible parses of a word form, reporting an F_1-score of 0.92. The authors report that the recall was far lower than the precision, indicating difficulty in learning to return all the valid parses. The problem of unsystematic ambiguity, however, can often be avoided in the parsing of verbs in polysynthetic languages with mostly systematic ambiguity. Navajo, for example, collapses singulars and duoplurals in the 3rd and 4th person, and so the ambiguity between the two could be encoded by introducing an additional super-tag representing both options at once.[2] In other words, systematic multiple readings can be circumvented in systems designed to give a single parse by simply altering the tagset for relevant cases, such that a parse with the tag [SG/DPL] could be interpreted as a two-way ambiguity. Another example is seen in Algonquian languages, which often have homophonous participle forms of verbs—affixes expressing features of the possessor are often homophonous with affixes expressing features of the subject or object.[3]

3   The Arapaho Verb

Arapaho is a member of the Algonquian (and larger Algic) language family; it is an agglutinating, polysynthetic language, with free word order (Cowell and Moss Sr, 2008). The language has a very complex verbal inflection system, with a number of typologically uncommon elements. Verb stems have unique stem-final elements which specify for valency and animacy: a given stem is used either with animate or inanimate subjects for intransitive verbs (**tei'eihi-** 'be strong.animate' vs. **tei'oo-** 'be strong.inanimate'), and with animate or inanimate objects for transitive verbs (**noohow-** 'see s.o.' vs. **noohoot-** 'see s.t.'). For each of these categories of stems, the pronominal affixes/inflections that attach to the verb stem vary in form, for example, 2SG with intransitive, animate subject verbs is **/-n/**, while for transitive, inanimate object verbs it is **/-ow/** (**nih-tei'eihi-n** 'you were strong' vs. **nih-noohoot-ow** 'you saw it').

All of these stem types can occur in four different verbal orders, whose function is primarily modal—affirmative, conjunct/subordinate, imperative, and non-affirmative. These verbal orders each use different pronominal affixes/inflections as well. For example, when a verbal root such as **/nooh /** 'see' is transitive with an animate object, 2SG acting on 3SG is **/-in/** or **/-un/** for the imperative order (**noohow-un** '(you) see him!'), but **/-ot/** for the affirmative order (**nih-noohow-ot** 'you saw him'), and with the non-affirmative order the 2SG marker is a prefix, **/he-/**, not a suffix. Thus, with four different verb stem types and four different verbal orders, there are a total of 16 different potential inflectional paradigms for any verbal root, though there is some overlap in the paradigms, and not all stem forms are possible for all roots.

---

[2] The fourth person in Navajo is the form for an obligatorily human "impersonal" third person participant (Akmajian and Anderson, 1970; Young and Morgan, 1987).

[3] Thank you to an anonymous reviewer for this example.

Two final complications are vowel harmony with related consonant mutation, and a proximate/obviative system. Arapaho has both progressive and regressive vowel harmony, operating on /i/ and /e/ respectively. This results in alternations in both the inflections themselves, and the final elements of stems, such as **noohow-un** 'see him' vs. **niiteheib-in** 'help him', or **nih-ni'eeneb-e3en** 'I liked you' vs. **nih-ni'eenow-oot** 'he liked her'. Arapaho also has a proximate/obviative system, which does not overlap with either subject/object or agent/patient categories, but instead designates pragmatically more- and less-prominent participants. There are "direction-of-action" markers (elsewhere, for simplicity, we use "subject" and "object") included in inflections, which do not correspond to true pronominal affixes. Thus **nih-noohow-oot** 'more important 3SG saw less important 3S/PL' vs. **nih-noohob-eit** 'less important 3SG/PL saw more important 3S', and **nih-noohob-einoo** 'less important 3S saw more important 1S'. The elements **-oo-** and **-ei-** specify direction of action, not specific persons or numbers of participants. some of these suffixes produce systematic ambiguity, as shown in Table

Some "direction-of-action" markers generate ambiguity in person and number of the verb's arguments. Thus, for example, in **nih-noohob-eit** 'less important 3SG/PL saw more important 3SG' the /-eit/ suffix is systematically ambiguous as to the number of the less important/obviative 3rd-person participant.

4   Finite-State Model

A morphological analyzer is a prerequisite for many NLP tasks. It is even more crucial to have such a parser for morphologically complex languages such as Arapaho. A finite state transducer (FST) is the standard technology for creating morphological analyzers. The FST is bidirectional and able to simultaneously parse given inflected word forms and generate all possible word forms for a given stem (Beesley and Karttunen, 2003).

The Arapaho FST model used in this paper was constructed with the *foma* finite-state toolkit (Hulden, 2009). The FST is constructed in two parts, the first being a specification of the lexicon and morphotactics using the finite-state lexicon compiler (lexc). This is a high-level declarative language for effective lexicon creation, where concatenative morphological rules and morphological irregularities are addressed (Karttunen, 1993).

The second part implements the morphophonological rules of the language using "rewrite rules" that apply the appropriate changes in specified contexts. This way, the generated inflected word form is not merely a bundle of morphemes, but the completely correct form in accord with the morphophonological rules of the language. So, by applying, in a particular order (specified in the grammar of the language), the rewrite rules to the parsed forms generated in the lexc file, the result is a single FST able to both generate and parse. Figure 1 shows how the FST is designed to generate and parse an example.

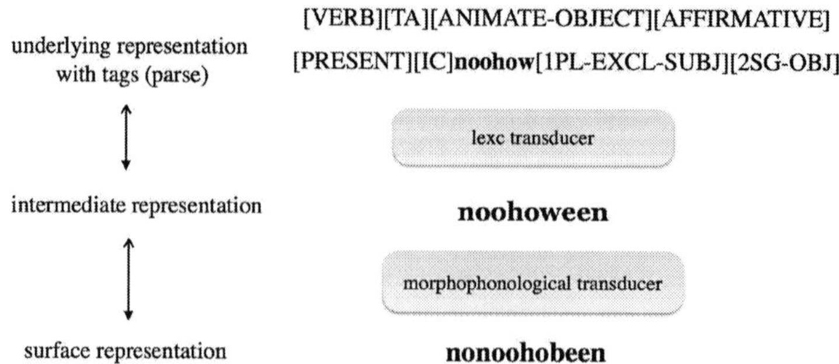

Figure 1: Composition in an FST illustrating the underlying (input) parsed forms and the resulting surface (output) inflected forms after mapping morpheme tags to concrete morphemes and subsequently undergoing morphophonological alternations.

The generalized application of rewrite application such that a FST or a neural model based on an

FST which is described below may seem like a "manufacturing" of the language, applying grammatical rules to verbal stems in order to create artificial forms. However, a morphological analyzer works with inflections and various kinds of prefixes; it does not build new verb stems. For the most part, it is the stems themselves that encode culture-sensitive information and perspectives.

5 Training a recurrent neural network from an FST

Tag	Description	Tag	Description
1PL-EXCL	First Person Plural Exclusive	1PL-INCL	First Person Plural Inclusive
3	Third Person Proximate	4	Third Person Obviative
II	Inanimate Subject Intransitive Verb	AI	Animate Subject Intransitive Verb
TI	Inanimate Object Transitive Verb	TA	Animate Object Transitive Verb
IC	Initial Change		

Table 1: Description of non-self-explanatory tags used in the parser

For training data, we extract inflected word forms and their corresponding parsed forms generated by the FST model for Arapaho, i.e. pairs such as the one seen at the top of Figure 1. These pairs serve as supervised examples to train a recurrent neural network (RNN) encoder-decoder. The set of FST-extracted input-output pairs contains 584,574 examples; however, a few forms had been incorrectly stored in the database and had to be identified and filtered before training. We trained on 60% of the filtered pairs. Another 20% was withheld for validation and an additional 20% as the test set. We evaluate the ability of the RNN to provide correct parses to unseen inflected word forms.

Since the currently strongest performing models for the related task of morphological inflection (Cotterell et al., 2017; Kann et al., 2017; Makarov et al., 2017) use an LSTM-based sequence-to-sequence (seq2seq) model (Sutskever et al., 2014), we follow this design in our work. Following Kann et al. (2017) who found that adding an attention mechanism (Bahdanau et al., 2015) improved performance, we always include attention as well. We treat parsing as a translation task of input character sequences from the fully-inflected surface forms to an output sequence of morphosyntactic tags plus the character sequences of the verbal root, i.e. we treat the root as the citation form to be retrieved. We implement the bidirectional LSTM-based sequence to sequence model with OpenNMT (Klein et al., 2017), using the default parameters that employ 2 layers for both the encoder and decoder, a hidden size of 500 for the recurrent unit, and a maximum batch size of 64. We train the model until the perplexity converges (at 1.02 or 1.01 for ambiguous and combined data, and 1.00 for unambiguous data), which usually occurs within 5 epochs and generally does not improve significantly with additional epochs. We experimented adding additional layers but without noticeable difference in the results.

As previous authors (Sutskever et al., 2014) have documented a sensitivity to element ordering, we experimented with training the model using various relative orders of morphosyntactic tags and the root morpheme: `Tags+Root`, `Root+Tags`, `Tags+Root+Tags`. These orders are shown in Table 2. (Table 1 provides the description of tags used in the parser that may not be self-explanatory).

Only the `Tags+Root` order was able to produce a model that parses any single inflected form completely correct. Examining the results of the `Tags+Root` predictions revealed that a majority of the mistakes involve the final letter of the root. The model often incorrectly predicts the last letter of the root morpheme, leaves it out completely, or adds an additional letter. Using an end-of-sequence marker does not affect this tendency, which we did not investigate further as we were able to avoid its effect by simply altering the order of the `Tags+Root` elements and the evaluation process. First, we trained the model with a `Tags+Root+Tags`[4] order, duplicating the morphosyntactic tags on both sides or the root, in the order that they were generated by the FST. After training, we removed the set of tags following the root and evaluated the neural encoder-decoder's predictions only against `Tags+Root` ordering of the test set.

---

[4] Repeating the Tags

Order	Example
Tags+Root	[VERB][TA][ANIMATE-OBJECT][AFFIRMATIVE][PRESENT][IC][1PL-EXCL-SUBJ][2SG-OBJ]**noohow**
Root+Tags	**noohow**[VERB][TA][ANIMATE-OBJECT][AFFIRMATIVE][PRESENT][IC][1PL-EXCL-SUBJ][2SG-OBJ]
Tags+Root+Tags	[VERB][TA][ANIMATE-OBJECT][AFFIRMATIVE][PRESENT][IC][1PL-EXCL-SUBJ][2SG-OBJ]**noohow**[VERB][TA][ANIMATE-OBJECT][AFFIRMATIVE][PRESENT][IC][1PL-EXCL-SUBJ][2SG-OBJ]

Table 2: Examples of orders of morphosyntactic tags and roots used for training the neural model. For encoder-decoder training, spaces were placed between square brackets and individual letters of the root. Thus, tags and letters were treated as single units for "translation".

Once high accuracy was reached on inflected word forms with only one possible parse, the ambiguous wordforms were added to the data. With no adjustments made to the output of the FST, the model parsed 46% of the test data completely correct. Removing all ambiguous surface forms which have than one possible parse increased the accuracy to 60%. With this setup, the accuracy for parsing full words did not exceed 60% without adjustments made for ambiguous words, the overall F_1-scores on individual tags and characters averaged over 0.9, indicating that, although 40% of the predicted parses contained at least one mistake, very few mistakes were made per wordform. Ambiguous forms were "disambiguated" for parsing by altering the tagset. Multiple morphosyntactic tags that are generated by one morpheme became a single tag containing generic information. For example, the word **nih-noohob-eit** 'less important 3SG/PL saw more important 3SG' has two possible parses. Its **/-eit/** suffix is systematically ambiguous as to the number of the less important/obviative 3rd-person participant. So the tagset substituted the two alternative parses—[3SG-SUBJ][3SG-OBJ] or [3PL-SUBJ][3SG-OBJ]— with a single new tag [3-SUBJ.3SG-OBJ]. Altering the tagset like this makes the predicted parsed forms less informative, since morphosyntactic information is lost for the sake of generalization. However, the predicted parses are no less ambiguous than are the corresponding fully-inflected Arapaho words when removed from context.

6 Results

Ambiguous and unambiguous word forms combined produce a training data size of about 245,600 supervised pairs. A little over half of those have unambiguous parses, but the actual percentage of unambiguous forms proffered by Arapaho's polysynthetic verbal inflection is probably closer to 75% because repeated ambiguous forms were not eliminated from the data. The RNN model was trained to produce root morphemes and morphosyntactic tags from fully-inflected word forms. The most accurate results came from training the model with morphosyntactic tags repeated before and after the root morpheme and removing the final set of tags before evaluating the model's prediction on the test set (Tags+Root+Tags ⇒ Tags+Root). Training only on unambiguous wordforms resulted in a final accuracy of 98.68%. After ambiguous forms were added to the data and the tagset was altered to "disambiguate" systematic alternative parses, the model's accuracy dropped from to 92.90%. This is better than the model's predictions of the ambiguous pairs on their own: 88.06%. The results of the model's prediction on individual tags and letters are broken down in the Appendix.

The nearly 93% accuracy is obtained by minimal disambiguation of ambiguous word forms. We removed specification of person and number from some arguments to account for the ambiguity of "direction-of-action" morphemes. The relatively low scores on certain tags, as shown in the Appendix, indicate that this accounts for only part of Arapaho's verbal morphological ambiguity. Other morphosyntactic information is ambiguous or, at least, more difficult to identify. For example, the difference between some transitive and intransitive verbs. Also, even some of the altered "direction-of-action" tags could be altered to become even less generic. Pre-processing should identify these morphemes and replace the alternative parses with as accurate a super-tag as the language's ambiguity allows. Such further disambiguation is a longer tail for future work, undoubtedly complicated by morphophonemic changes.

7   Discussion

Since even an endangered language expands and changes, a morphological analyzer that generalizes to unseen inflected forms is more useful than one that does not. Handwritten rules cannot reach into the long tail of lexicon expansion and difficult corner cases. The neural encoder-decoder model described in this paper overcomes the limitations of FST and handwritten rules. One advantage of an FST is the large number of surface and parsed pairs it generates for supervised training of our neural model. We paid attention to the best ordering of the morphosyntactic tags and verbal roots in the training data and found the best combination was training on Tags+Root+Tags and evaluating on Tags+Root. Our neural model can generalize with nearly 93% accuracy beyond what is explicitly encoded. This result comes in part from the lack of systematic ambiguity in a polysynthetic language such as Arapaho, but future work should increase the usefulness of the parses by handling ambiguities beyond person/number, and handling those with more precision. Although some of our experiments trained on random small percentages of the FST-generated data, further refinement and reduction of the data would demonstrate how the neural model performs on an incomplete selection of word forms, a situation not uncommon from hand-written descriptions of endangered languages.[5]

References

Adrian Akmajian and Stephen Anderson. 1970. On the use of fourth person in Navajo, or Navajo made harder. *International Journal of American Linguistics*, 36(1):1–8.

Dzmitry Bahdanau, Kyunghyun Cho, and Yoshua Bengio. 2015. Neural machine translation by jointly learning to align and translate. In *ICLR*.

Kenneth R. Beesley and Lauri Karttunen. 2003. *Finite State Morphology*. CSLI Publications, Stanford, CA.

Ryan Cotterell, Christo Kirov, John Sylak-Glassman, David Yarowsky, Jason Eisner, and Mans Hulden. 2016. The SIGMORPHON 2016 shared task—morphological reinflection. In *Proceedings of the 14th SIGMOR-PHON Workshop on Computational Research in Phonetics, Phonology, and Morphology*, pages 10–22, Berlin, Germany, August. Association for Computational Linguistics.

Ryan Cotterell, Christo Kirov, John Sylak-Glassman, Géraldine Walther, Ekaterina Vylomova, Patrick Xia, Man-aal Faruqui, Sandra Kübler, David Yarowsky, Jason Eisner, and Mans Hulden. 2017. CoNLL-SIGMORPHON 2017 shared task: Universal morphological reinflection in 52 languages. In *Proceedings of the CoNLL SIG-MORPHON 2017 Shared Task: Universal Morphological Reinflection*, pages 1–30. Association for Computational Linguistics.

Andrew Cowell and Alonzo Moss Sr. 2008. *The Arapaho Language*. University Press of Colorado.

Mans Hulden. 2009. Foma: a finite-state compiler and library. In *Proceedings of the 12th Conference of the European Chapter of the Association for Computational Linguistics*, pages 29–32. Association for Computational Linguistics.

Katharina Kann, Ryan Cotterell, and Hinrich Schütze. 2017. Neural multi-source morphological reinflection. In *Proceedings of the 15th Conference of the European Chapter of the Association for Computational Linguistics: Volume 1, Long Papers*, pages 514–524. Association for Computational Linguistics.

Lauri Karttunen. 1993. *Finite-state lexicon compiler*. Xerox Corporation. Palo Alto Research Center.

Ghazaleh Kazeminejad, Andrew Cowell, and Mans Hulden. 2017. Creating lexical resources for polysynthetic languages—the case of Arapaho. In *Proceedings of the 2nd Workshop on the Use of Computational Methods in the Study of Endangered Languages*, pages 10–18, Honolulu, March. Association for Computational Linguistics.

[5] We gratefully acknowledge the support of NVIDIA Corporation with the donation of the Titan Xp GPU used for this research.

G. Klein, Y. Kim, Y. Deng, J. Senellart, and A. M. Rush. 2017. OpenNMT: Open-Source Toolkit for Neural Machine Translation. *ArXiv e-prints*.

Kimmo Koskenniemi. 1983. *Two-level morphology: A general computational model for word-form recognition and production*. Publication 11, University of Helsinki, Department of General Linguistics, Helsinki.

Krister Lindén, Miikka Silfverberg, and Tommi Pirinen. 2009. HFST tools for morphology—an efficient open-source package for construction of morphological analyzers. In *International Workshop on Systems and Frameworks for Computational Morphology*, pages 28–47. Springer.

Peter Makarov, Tatiana Ruzsics, and Simon Clematide. 2017. Align and copy: UZH at SIGMORPHON 2017 shared task for morphological reinflection. In *Proceedings of the CoNLL SIGMORPHON 2017 Shared Task: Universal Morphological Reinflection*, pages 49–57, Vancouver, August. Association for Computational Linguistics.

Michael Maxwell. 2015. Grammar debugging. In *Systems and Frameworks for Computational Morphology*, pages 166–183. Springer.

Miikka Silfverberg and Mans Hulden. 2018. Initial experiments in data-driven morphological analysis for Finnish. In *Proceedings of the Fourth International Workshop on Computatinal Linguistics of Uralic Languages*, pages 100–107, Helsinki, Finland, January. Association for Computational Linguistics.

Ilya Sutskever, Oriol Vinyals, and Quoc V. Le. 2014. Sequence to sequence learning with neural networks. In *Advances in Neural Information Processing Systems (NIPS)*, pages 3104–3112.

Robert Young and William Morgan. 1987. *The Navajo Language: a Grammar and Colloquial Dictionary*. University of New Mexico Press, Albuquerque.

8 Appendix

Below are the results from training the neural model to produce disambiguated morphosyntactic tags both before and after a root morpheme, but evaluated only on the first set of tags and the root morpheme. The training model works with a vocabulary of 56 morphosyntactic tags and 16 letters. The 80/20/20 train/dev/test split resulted in 81,883 test examples of both ambiguous and unambiguous forms.

Tag or Letter	Precision	Recall	F_1-score	Instances
[1PL-EXCL-SUBJ.2PL-OBJ]	0.96	0.99	0.98	1381
[1PL-EXCL-SUBJ.2SG-OBJ]	1.00	0.99	0.99	1413
[1PL-EXCL-SUBJ.3PL-OBJ]	0.66	0.99	0.79	1395
[1PL-EXCL-SUBJ.3SG-OBJ]	1.00	0.50	0.66	1397
[1PL-INCL-SUBJ.3-OBJ]	0.98	1.00	0.99	2759
[1PL-INCL-SUBJ]	0.99	0.98	0.98	712
[1PL-SUBJ]	1.00	0.99	1.00	1396
[1SG-SUBJ]	0.98	0.98	0.98	673
[1SG-SUBJ][2PL-OBJ]	1.00	1.00	1.00	1407
[1SG-SUBJ][2SG-OBJ]	0.99	1.00	1.00	1350
[1SG-SUBJ][3PL-OBJ]	0.85	0.99	0.91	1363
[1SG-SUBJ][3SG-OBJ]	0.88	0.98	0.93	1384
[2PL-SUBJ.3-OBJ]	0.99	0.99	0.99	4085
[2PL-SUBJ]	0.98	0.97	0.97	1394
[2PL-SUBJ][1PL-EXCL-OBJ]	1.00	1.00	1.00	2020
[2PL-SUBJ][1SG-OBJ]	0.96	0.98	0.97	2078
[2SG-SUBJ]	1.00	0.83	0.91	1052
[2SG-SUBJ][1PL-EXCL-OBJ]	1.00	1.00	1.00	2082
[2SG-SUBJ][1SG-OBJ]	0.89	0.95	0.92	2057
[2SG-SUBJ][3PL-OBJ]	0.99	0.68	0.80	2099
[2SG-SUBJ][3SG-OBJ]	0.73	0.98	0.84	2047
[3-SUBJ.1PL-INCL-OBJ]	0.99	0.99	0.99	2751
[3-SUBJ.2PL-OBJ]	0.99	0.99	0.99	2829
[3-SUBJ.4-OBJ]	0.98	0.99	0.99	2802
[3PL-SUBJ.4-OBJ]	0.99	0.99	0.99	2767
[3PL-SUBJ]	0.99	0.85	0.91	2600
[3PL-SUBJ][1PL-EXCL-OBJ]	0.69	0.93	0.79	1352
[3PL-SUBJ][1SG-OBJ]	0.98	0.99	0.98	1351
[3PL-SUBJ][2SG-OBJ]	1.00	1.00	1.00	1384
[3SG-SUBJ]	0.98	0.81	0.89	2614
[3SG-SUBJ][1PL-EXCL-OBJ]	0.90	0.57	0.70	1344
[3SG-SUBJ][1SG-OBJ]	0.98	1.00	0.99	1298
[3SG-SUBJ][2SG-OBJ]	0.99	1.00	1.00	1401
[4-SUBJ.3PL-OBJ]	0.99	0.99	0.99	2867
[4 SUBJ.3SG OBJ]	0.99	0.99	0.99	2788
[4-SUBJ.4-OBJ]	0.99	1.00	0.99	11016
[4PL-SUBJ]	0.95	0.98	0.97	2630
[4SG-SUBJ]	0.93	0.96	0.94	2545
[AFFIRMATIVE]	1.00	1.00	1.00	36878
[AI]	0.84	0.90	0.87	1144
[ANIMATE-OBJECT]	0.99	1.00	0.99	66267
[ANIMATE-SUBJECT]	0.84	0.90	0.87	1144
[IC]	1.00	0.99	0.99	18417

Continued on next page

Table 3 – Continued from previous page

Tag or Letter	Precision	Recall	F$_1$-score	Instances
[II]	0.98	0.93	0.95	6547
[IMPERATIVE]	0.95	0.98	0.97	3124
[INANIMATE-OBJECT]	0.99	0.92	0.95	7935
[INANIMATE-SUBJECT]	0.98	0.93	0.95	6547
[INTERROGATIVE]	1.00	1.00	1.00	19884
[NEG]	1.00	1.00	1.00	18850
[NON _ AFFIRMATIVE]	1.00	1.00	1.00	38734
[PAST]	1.00	1.00	1.00	18461
[PRESENT]	1.00	1.00	1.00	57151
[PROHIBITIVE]	1.00	1.00	1.00	3157
[TA]	0.99	1.00	0.99	66267
[TI]	0.99	0.92	0.95	7935
[VERB]	1.00	1.00	1.00	81893
b	0.95	0.99	0.97	19171
c	1.00	1.00	1.00	18440
e	0.99	0.99	0.99	85704
h	1.00	0.99	1.00	61047
i	0.99	0.99	0.99	103323
k	1.00	1.00	1.00	21331
n	0.99	0.99	0.99	71447
o	0.99	0.99	0.99	157112
s	1.00	0.99	0.99	17716
t	1.00	0.99	0.99	34310
u	0.99	1.00	0.99	38280
w	0.98	0.95	0.96	22060
x	0.99	0.99	0.99	14429
y	0.99	0.99	0.99	6978
'	1.00	1.00	1.00	35888
3	0.99	1.00	1.00	31242
average/total:	0.97	0.96	0.96	1,280,696

Finite-state morphology for Kwak'wala:
A phonological approach

Patrick Littell
National Research Council of Canada
1200 Montreal Road, Ottawa ON, K1A 0R6
`patrick.littell@nrc.gc.ca`

Abstract

This paper presents the phonological layer of a Kwak'wala finite-state morphological transducer, using the phonological hypotheses of Lincoln and Rath (1986) and the "lenient composition" operation of Karttunen (1998) to mediate the complicated relationship between underlying and surface forms. The resulting system decomposes the wide variety of surface forms in such a way that the morphological layer can be specified using unique and largely concatenative morphemes.

1   Introduction

Kwak'wala[1] (ISO 639-3: kwk) is a Northern Wakashan language of British Columbia, spoken primarily on the northern part of Vancouver Island, the adjacent mainland, and the islands in between. Kwak'wala morphology and morphophonology is famously complex; words are frequently made up of many morphemes, and these morphemes can cause dramatic changes in the surface realizations of words.

As a basic example, the root for "man" can occur in various forms depending on the suffixes with which it occurs, and in some of these words (the three ending in -əm) the identity of the suffix can *only* be distinguished by the effects (lenition, fortition, vowel lengthening, or reduplication) that it has on the root:

(1)	bəgʷanəm	"man"
	bagʷans	"visitor" (literally, "unexpected man")
	bəkʷəm	"without expression, sternly" (literally, "man-face") (FirstVoices, 2009)
	bək̓ʷəs	"Wildman of the forest"
	bak̓ʷəm	"First Nations person" (literally, "genuine man")
	babagʷom	"boy"

This is compounded by suffixes potentially changing syllable structure as well, which further increases the apparent variety of surface forms:

(2)	de	"to wipe" (Boas et al., 1947)
	dixʔid	"to wipe something" (FirstVoices, 2009)
	dayax̌stənd	"to wipe one's mouth" (FirstVoices, 2009)
	dəʔełbənd	"to wipe one's nose" (FirstVoices, 2009)

The combination of mutation and resyllabification can cause a complete restructuring of the word. For example, adding the participial suffix -ł to the root pix̌ʷ- ("feel") results not in something like [*pix̌ʷł] but rather [pəyuł], in which only the first and last letters remain intact.

---

[1] Strictly speaking, Kwak'wala is the most-spoken variety of a larger language for which there is no completely-agreed-upon name. This language is often also called Kwak'wala, but some speakers prefer a more general term Bak'wəmk'ala (Littell, 2016, pp. 29–30).

Proceedings of Workshop on Polysynthetic Languages, pages 21–30
Santa Fe, New Mexico, USA, August 20-26, 2018.

(3)

pix̌ʷ ("feel")	+ ł (participle)	= pəyuł ("felt") (Boas et al., 1947)
məx̌ʷ ("desire")	+ ł (participle)	= muł ("desired") (Boas et al., 1947)
gʷas ("chap")	+ ł (participle)	= gʷeł ("chapped") (Boas et al., 1947)
kʷəns ("bake bread")	+ kʷ (nominal)	= kʷənikʷ ("bread")
xʷas ("excite")	+ kʷ (nominal)	= xʷekʷ ("excited") (Boas et al., 1947)
guł ("eat while traveling")	+ kʷ (nominal)	= gəwəlkʷ ("food for travel") (Boas et al., 1947)

Given such changes, a grammar engineer has two potential avenues of approach to Kwak'wala morphology:

1. Assume that Kwak'wala has a fairly straightforward relationship between phonemes and surface phones, but that roots and suffixes fall into a large number of derivational classes that behave differently when certain suffixes are added.

2. Assume that Kwak'wala has a comparatively straightforward agglutinative morphology, with morphemes that have unique forms and are mostly separable at the phonemic level, and that the apparent diversity of surface forms is due to a complex phonological component.

The FST described in this paper leans towards the second approach, meaning that the lion's share of the difficult work will be in the phonological component, while the morphological component should be (mostly) concatenative and assume (where possible) one unique form for each morpheme. Given this, this paper concentrates on creating the phonological component, the success or failure of which determines what form the morphological component must take. The phonological component uses the "lenient composition" technique of Karttunen (1998) to express Kwak'wala phonology in an Optimality-Theoretic way, while maintaining the linear-time efficiency of a finite-state system. This is, to our knowledge, the first attempt at computationalizing Kwak'wala morphophonology.

The downside of the phonological approach here is that there are few people who have a mastery of this particular style of Northern Wakashan phonological analysis, and thus while the resulting system is simpler, it can be difficult even for someone familiar with Kwak'wala to look at the resulting grammar and understand what is going on. To try to mitigate this, we are attempting to write this grammar in a "literate" (in the sense of Knuth (1992) and Maxwell (2012)) style, with a greater proportion of human-readable prose accompanied by relatively short snippets of executable code.

2 Motivation

Wä, laᵉlaĕ â'laɛl pâ'lĕda ᵉwä'latsɛma.
Wä, laɛ'mᵉlaĕ hĕ'mɛnałaɛm ᵉnɛmō'-
kwĕda pō'sdanäxa ᵉnĕᵉnä'la. Wä, lä'ᵉlaĕ
yä'q!eg·ałĕda ᵉnɛmō'kwĕ lax aᵉyî'lkwäs
Qa'wadiliqala lä'xĕs g·ō'kulōtĕ. Lä'ᵉlaĕ
ᵉnĕ'k·a : "ᵉyä'x·daᵉxᵘ, wä'ɛntsōs hō'ʟĕla
g·ä'xɛn, g·ō'kulōt, qaɛn yä'q!ĕg·ałĕsg·a
gwä'łaä'sg·asg·în nâ'qĕk·. Wä, hĕ'ᵉmɛn
nâ'qaᵉĕda, qɛns lä hō'gwɪʟ lax g·ō'-
kwasa g·ɪ'gamaᵉyaɛns, qaɛ'ns ha'waʟɪ'-
lagâ'lĕ qɛns g·ä'yuʟasɛ'x haᵉmä'ᵉya."

Figure 1: An excerpt from Boas and Hunt (1902). The stories, songs, history, and oratory collected by Boas and Hunt constitute a substantial body of text—still the largest corpus of Kwak'wala—and contain much that is of cultural and linguistic interest to this day. However, few modern readers can read this orthography.

The FST described in this paper is intended as part of a spell-checking system, initially intended to help guide the optical character recognition (OCR) of historical texts (e.g. Boas and Hunt (1902)). There are extensive high-quality scans of documents from the early 20th century, but they are written in an orthography that most modern readers find impenetrable. OCR is the first step to unlocking this content for modern readers.[2] It may also be the case that the resulting spellchecker can be useful for end-users (e.g. in a word processor) and other downstream tasks.

Since we do not have a complete lexicon of Kwak'wala, we cannot at this point design a system that divides *actual* Kwak'wala words from *non-actual* ones. Rather, this system has to divide *possible* Kwak'wala words from *impossible* ones.

This is, however, probably much of what we want a low-resource spell-checker to do. We do not want to limit an OCR system for historical texts, for example, to words known in the modern era; part of the reason for engaging with these texts is to rediscover words that are no longer commonly used. We do, however, want to avoid hypothesizing forms that *could not* be Kwak'wala words.

The morphophonological complexity of Kwak'wala presents an opportunity here, and not just a challenge. Because the morphophonology shapes words in particular ways, given an unknown word we can, with some degree of confidence, (1) guess that it *is* a Kwak'wala word and (2) have some idea of its structure, even if its meaning, and the meaning of its components, are unclear. For example, even if we do not know that the following word means "school", we can determine from its shape that it probably is a Kwak'wala word (not a loanword, or a sequence of random characters, or an OCR error) and that it has four or five component morphemes (because it contains three or four phoneme sequences that we associate with changes that happen across morpheme boundaries).

(4) q̓aq̓uƛ̓əʔac̓i
     q̓a-q̓awƛ-_sa-as-_si
     try-know-try-LOC-NOMINAL

     "school" (literally: "building where one learns")

3 A phonological approach to the complexity of Kwak'wala morphology

Kwak'wala is noted for its highly complex morphology and morphophonology, and is, by the definition of polysynthesis in Anderson (1985), the prototypical polysynthetic language.[3] There are roughly 400–500 suffixal or enclitic elements that can be added to roots, many of which (the "lexical suffixes") have quite concrete meanings of the sort that few languages (outside of the Wakashan and some neighboring languages) express in suffixes. These suffixes express body parts, different sorts of ground the action is done on (e.g. on the beach, on manmade surfaces, in a forest, in a boat, etc.), shapes, paths of motion, and even different kinds of physical technology (e.g. tools vs. containers vs. work surfaces vs. headgear). In addition to this, there is also a layer of inflectional morphology, and beyond this a tendency for all small particle-like words that follow the word to encliticize to the previous word.[4]

On top of this, Kwak'wala phonology and morphophonology is also highly complex, with suffixes causing a variety of mutations (particularly fortition and lenition) in the bases to which they attach. These mutations can then interact with the syllabification, stress, and vowel derivation systems to cause surprising alternations, as in (3).

In order to compartmentalize this complexity, we assume a phonology roughly equivalent to that of Lincoln and Rath (1980) and Lincoln and Rath (1986), which posited that Northern Wakashan words consist underlyingly of sequences of consonants (e.g. /pyx̌ʷɬ/ for [pəyuɬ] and /kʷnskʷ/ for [kʷənikʷ]),

---

[2]The second step, conversion between historical and modern orthographies, is already available at orth.nfshost.com, although this component will probably also undergo further development with the flood of new historical text that will become available due to OCR.

[3]It depends, however, on which definition of polysynthesis one uses. Anderson's definition (which comes out of his own research on Kwak'wala) only requires that the language typically expresses within words what other languages require whole sentences for. On the other hand, if we take the definition of polysynthesis in Baker (1996), which requires verbal inflection for particular structural arguments, Kwak'wala is probably not polysynthetic; much of the complexity of Kwak'wala morphology is probably not *inflectional* per se and does not necessarily involve the arguments intended by Baker.

[4]Kwak'wala also has famously complex reduplication patterns (Struijke, 1998; Struijke, 2000), but this system does not yet attempt to account for them.

which are vocalized by the epenthesis of schwas and the realization of particular consonants as syllabic nuclei (here, the lenition of /x̌ʷ/ to /w/ and /s/ to /y/, respectively, and their subsequent vocalization to [u] and [i]). Since suffixes affect syllabification and can mutate consonants (and thus change their potential vocalizations), different root+suffix combinations can appear to have dramatically different surface forms.

4 Implementation

The phonological transducer is written in the `Foma` (Hulden, 2009) implementation of the XFST language (Beesley and Karttunen, 2003). More specifically, it is written using the Python bindings for Foma, allowing the automation of boilerplate code in Python and the use of Jupyter for "literate programming" (Knuth, 1992; Maxwell and Amith, 2005; Maxwell, 2012) (Fig. 2).

▾ Consonant inventory

Kwak'wala has a rich inventory of consonants, but not all of them have similar distributions. There are two important distinctions in the consonants:

- **"Plain" vs. "special" consonants**: Plain consonants (mostly voiceless plosives, fricatives, and non-glottalized resonants) can occur almost anywhere in a word, and the sound changes they undergo are regular and largely predictable. Special consonants (voiced and ejective plosives and glottalized resonants), on the other hand, are rare to find morpheme-finally, and do not mutate in the same way as plain consonants do.

- **Resonant vs. non-resonant consonants**: There is also a division between non-glottalized resonant consonants (/m/, /n/, /l/, /y/, /w/) and all other consonants. In particular, non-glottalized resonant consonants can occupy syllabic nuclei (with many consequences to syllabification, stress, and reduplication), and various morphophonological changes apply only to resononant consonants.

Implementation: The code below defines four new symbols, corresponding to the four possibilities with respect to the above distinctions. The right side of each assignment is a disjunction; as an example, the first one means "it's a [p], or it's a [t], or it's a [c], etc." Defining these four new symbols lets us just say "PlainNonRes" every time we want to refer to this class, rather than having to enumerate the possibilities every time.

```
[85]    1 definitions["PlainNonRes"]    = "[p|t|c|ƛ|k|kʷ|q|qʷ|s|f|v|ł|x|xʷ|x̌|x̌ʷ]"
        2 definitions["SpecialNonRes"]  = "[p̓|t̓|c̓|ƛ̓|k̓|k̓ʷ|q̓|q̓ʷ|ʔ|b|d|dz|λ|g|gʷ|ǧ|ǧʷ|h]"
        3 definitions["PlainResonant"]  = "[m|n|l|w|y]"
        4 definitions["SpecialResonant"] = "[m̓|n̓|l̓|w̓|y̓]"
```

Figure 2: Example of a "literate programming" style, which conceptualizes the primary consumer of code to be human (and thus interested in understanding either the code or the phenomenon that the code purports to capture), and augments this human-consumable description with pieces of machine-interpretable code (in this case XFST regular expressions, interpreted by Foma via a Python interface).

There is not currently a lexical component (e.g. an LEXC file filled with known morphemes); rather, a "guesser" allows any well-formed underlying form. In the future, this will be filled by a devoted lexical component, but since the structure of that component depends largely on whether this phonological component is successful, it has been left to future research. In this experiment, the underlying forms are drawn from a field corpus that includes proposals of underlying forms (§6.1).

5 Phonology and morphophonology in XFST

5.1 Phonetic and phonemic inventory

Kwak'wala has a large phonetic inventory and a complex phonology that is not yet completely understood (particularly concerning the vowel inventory). There are 42 consonants, all of which are underlying[5]. There are approximately 10-12 distinct vowel qualities, but this system follows most modern Kwak'wala

---

[5] It is possible that [h] is epenthetic, and may historically have been so, but it is not possible to posit that *both* [h] and [ə] are epenthetic due to words like [həmumu] ("butterfly"). Assuming that [ə] is always epenthetic has significant explanatory power for many otherwise-puzzling forms, so this system must assume that /h/ is underlying.

orthographies in representing six distinct surface vowels [ə, a, e, i, o, u]; the surface vowel qualities are almost entirely predictable from the orthographic form.

In a Lincoln and Rath-style (1980, 1986) Northern Wakashan phonology, underlying forms consist primarily of consonants and most vowels are derived (either epenthetic or derived from consonants). Unlike Lincoln and Rath, whose phonemicization is entirely consonantal, we allow three actual underlying vowels, /a/, /i/, and /u/, although all are marginal in some way. [i] and [u] are probably often underlyingly /y/ and /w/, but a few forms suggest that /i/~/y/ and /u/~/w/ cannot completely be unified, and we typically default to positing that surface [i] and [u] are underlyingly /i/ and /u/ unless there is specific evidence otherwise. Lincoln and Rath also posit that [a] is a realization of /h/; we instead treat it as a separate phoneme.

5.2 Orthography

Roughly six distinct Kwak'wala orthographies can be identified, in three families:

1. Two stages (early and late) of the orthography used by Boas and his collaborators, and seen in Fig. 1. Most modern readers cannot read this orthography.

2. Two similar orthographies based on Royal British Columbia Museum conventions. The more recent version of this style, called "U'mista" script after the U'mista Cultural Centre in Alert Bay, is the de facto standard for most communities, and is the orthography in which modern books are published.

3. Two variants of the Americanist Phonetic Alphabet, typically used by linguists in the region, and seen in this paper.

The example forms given in this paper are orthographic rather than phonetic, using the typical six orthographic vowels; specifically, this paper is written using the University of Victoria variant of the North American Phonetic Alphabet (NAPA). A caron indicates a uvular consonant, and an apostrophe above a letter represents glottalization; the barred lambda [ƛ] indicates a voiceless lateral affricate.

Although it is intended to be used mostly for documents written in (1)- or (2)-type orthographies, the transducer uses a NAPA orthography internally, because NAPA-type orthographies allow the unambiguous expression of Lincoln-and-Rath-style underlying forms, and allow the differentiation of all the sounds in the test corpus (§6.1).

5.3 Syllabification

For some languages, one can dispense with a detailed syllabification when writing a practical morphological FST, since one can define environments (like "onset") in terms of linear consonant/vowel phonotactics (e.g., "consonant before a vowel"). In Kwak'wala, it is crucial to determine the actual syllabification, because the entire word might consist of consonant phonemes; a phoneme will be *realized* as a consonant or a vowel depending on its syllabification, which can change depending on a variety of factors.

To determine syllable structure, we adopt an approach outlined in Karttunen (1998), in which Optimality Theory-like violable constraints (Prince and Smolensky, 1993) on syllable structure are implemented via the "lenient composition" of transducers.

A lenient composition X .O. Y acts as a regular composition X .o. Y when the range of X overlaps with the domain of Y; otherwise, X is used alone. This allows the expression of constraints that can be violated: they apply if they would produce output – that is, if there are some "live" candidates that would successfully pass their test – but if they would result in an empty set of outputs they do not apply.

5.4 Counting constraints

Much of the implementation complexity – and the resulting size of the network – comes from the necessity for some constraints to count how many violations of them occur.

For example, consider a DEP constraint ("don't epenthesize") against the epenthesis of schwas – call this "NoSchwa". We can compose this (by lenient composition) with our generator function GEN (which

```
define NoSchwa ~$[ schwa ] ;
define GRAMMAR GEN .O. NoSchwa
```

Figure 3: Example XFST code illustrating a constraint that *cannot* count the number of violations.

creates candidate forms) to exclude forms with schwas when schwa-less forms exist, but to allow forms with schwas when that is the only possibility (Fig. 3).

This is not, however, what we want from the system: we want it to *minimize* the number of schwas. The automaton above cannot count schwas; a word with two schwas (like ƛatəmɬ, "hat") is just as bad within this system as a word with three (like ƛatəmaɬ), so any input that successfully generates the correct form ƛatəmɬ will also generate every possible form with additional schwas like ƛatəmaɬ.

It is therefore necessary to compose constraints that *count* schwas (Fig. 4).

```
define NoSchwa0 ~$[ schwa ] ;
define NoSchwa1 ~[[$ schwa ]^>1] ;
define NoSchwa2 ~[[$ schwa ]^>2] ;
define NoSchwa3 ~[[$ schwa ]^>3] ;
define GRAMMAR GEN .O. NoSchwa .O. NoSchwa1 .O. NoSchwa2 .O. NoSchwa3 ;
```

Figure 4: Example XFST code illustrating constraints that can count violations.

Each of these constraints allows a specific number of schwas through, but no more. This allows us to capture the idea that violable constraints are sensitive to the number of violations; we can picture this implementation as a decomposition of the tableau on the left of Fig. 5 to the tableau on the right.

/ƛtmɬ/	NoSchwa
☞ [ƛatəmɬ]	**
[ƛatəmaɬ]	***

/ƛtmɬ/	NoSchwa0	NoSchwa1	NoSchwa2	NoSchwa3
☞ [ƛatəmɬ]	*	*	*	
[ƛatəmaɬ]	*	*	*	*

Figure 5: Left: An Optimality-Theoretic tableau illustrating how a form with fewer schwas is preferred over a form with more. Right: A representation of the actual implementation of this constraint in a finite-state system. The pointing finger indicates the "winning" candidate: the form that remains when all other forms have been excluded due to violating a higher-ranked constraint.

Since this is largely boilerplate code, we automate it by defining a slightly higher-level language in Python (e.g., a macro-style function `constrain("schwa", max=3)`) and then transpile that to code like that in Fig. 4.

6 Experiment and Results

In this paper, we evaluate the phonological transducer by considering whether it can generate the attested surface forms in a corpus that contains both surface (e.g. ƛatəmɬ) and proposed underlying (e.g. ƛtmɬ) forms.

We are primarily interested in recall here (how many of the attested surface forms the system can generate), but since the underlying-to-surface relationship in this corpus is one-to-many (there are multiple valid ways to transcribe a given form[6]), we also report precision and F1, as an attempt to avoid overgenerating and producing unattested surface forms.[7]

---

[6]There is little valid ambiguity, however, in how a surface form corresponds to an underlying form. There are many instances where the underlying form is *unclear* due to our incomplete understanding of the phonology, and many instances where the corpus happens to be inconsistent in how it presents underlying forms, but there are few if any instances in which different underlying forms happen to be pronounced identically.

[7]Although this transducer is scored on a somewhat "canned" dataset, it is still not possible to achieve 1.0 precision and F1; leaving aside errors in the corpus and loanwords that do not follow Kwak'wala phonology, there is genuine variation in

The documents in the corpus are divided into a 75% development set (on which we did error analysis while writing the grammar) and a 25% test set (which we did not look at), to test whether the rules proposed to handle the development set generalize to unseen documents.

6.1 Corpus

	Development set	Test set
Documents	230	77
Word types	4575	1490
Word tokens	12610	3317

Table 1: Document, type, and token counts for the development and test sets

This transducer was tested on our own fieldwork corpus, currently part of the private archives at the Whatcom Museum in Bellingham, WA, representing field interviews with eight speakers of Kwak'wala.

Each word in the corpus is given a proposed underlying form, although there is some variation in how these forms are presented. In particular, there are cases where morphemes are or are not separated, or distinctions that are or are not made, according to the purpose of this example. In addition, there are various morphemes whose status as a suffix or enclitic is unclear, and which may at different points be analyzed as either. For this reason, we are only interested here in evaluating the "downward" direction of the transducer (that is, generating possible orthographic surface forms from underlying forms), rather than the "upward" direction (that is, parsing surface forms into proposed underlying forms); the latter represents a set of changing conventions of little current practical interest.

6.2 Results and Discussion

Figure 6 gives the recall, precision, and F1 for the baseline system and a number of improvements to the phonological rules and constraints.

While this is more detail than is typically reported for grammar development, and the particular changes are probably of interest only to Wakashanist phonologists, we thought it was illustrative to show the progression of development. In particular, it illustrates that expert system development is not always hill-climbing, and some changes cause losses that are repaired only by later development; for example, the epenthesis of schwas leads to a large precision drop due to overgeneration, but many of these forms are later avoided by allowing a more complex syllable structure.

The baseline system only removes elements like word and morpheme boundaries, and makes no further changes in between the underlying form and the surface form. As the baseline system only has a recall of 30.6%, this means that about 69.4% of Kwak'wala word tokens[8] have a more complex syllable structure or undergo some sort of phonological or morphological change before surfacing.

Beyond the baseline, additional improvements to the phonological system typically made steady improvements to recall, and had various effects (positive and negative) on precision. We generally did not take a loss of precision to be necessarily bad, as typically many of the new forms predicted were indeed *possible* pronunciations of words, although not attested in this small corpus; a precision loss is something to investigate further here, but not necessarily reject a rule or constraint over.

Of special note is the spirantization of /ƛ/, /k/, /kʷ/, /q/, and /qʷ/ in syllable codas to [ł], [x], [xʷ], [x̌], and [x̌ʷ] respectively. This change is nearly (but not entirely) obligatory in the speech of our consultants, but historically it was more variable. Specifying this change as optional caused a noticeable drop in precision (as many of the predicted non-spirant forms are not attested in our modern corpus), but it is still valuable to allow them given that such forms *do* occur more frequently in historical texts.

Analysis of a sample of errors suggests that most are of two types: errors in the corpus itself, and phenomena that we had inadequately annotated in underlying forms (especially which initial phonemes

---

pronunciation (both free variation and variation between speakers) such that not every *possible* realization of an underlying form is attested in the corpus.

[8] At the word type level, the baseline system has a recall of 14.1%, meaning that about 85.9% of word types have more complex syllable structure or phonology.

System	Development set			Test set		
	Recall	Precision	F1	Recall	Precision	F1
Baseline system	0.306	0.595	0.404	0.288	0.558	0.380
Epenthesis of schwas	0.382	0.405	0.393	0.351	0.372	0.361
Avoid final schwas	0.382	0.436	0.408	0.351	0.400	0.374
Resonant and special nuclei	0.479	0.548	0.511	0.458	0.523	0.488
Additional coda possibilities	0.523	0.607	0.562	0.492	0.571	0.528
Monophthongize /aw, ay, aẃ, aẏ/	0.525	0.604	0.562	0.494	0.564	0.527
Fortition/lenition of plain consonants	0.589	0.576	0.582	0.561	0.539	0.550
Fortition/lenition special cases	0.599	0.582	0.590	0.573	0.548	0.560
Glottalization of ʔm, ʔl	0.633	0.586	0.609	0.610	0.561	0.584
Spirantization of /ƛ, k, kʷ, q, qʷ/ in codas	0.652	0.546	0.595	0.634	0.515	0.568
Avoiding resonant onsets	0.684	0.624	0.653	0.667	0.591	0.627
Morpheme-initial deletion	0.722	0.662	0.690	0.716	0.635	0.673
Hiatus resolution special cases	0.757	0.612	0.677	0.743	0.610	0.670

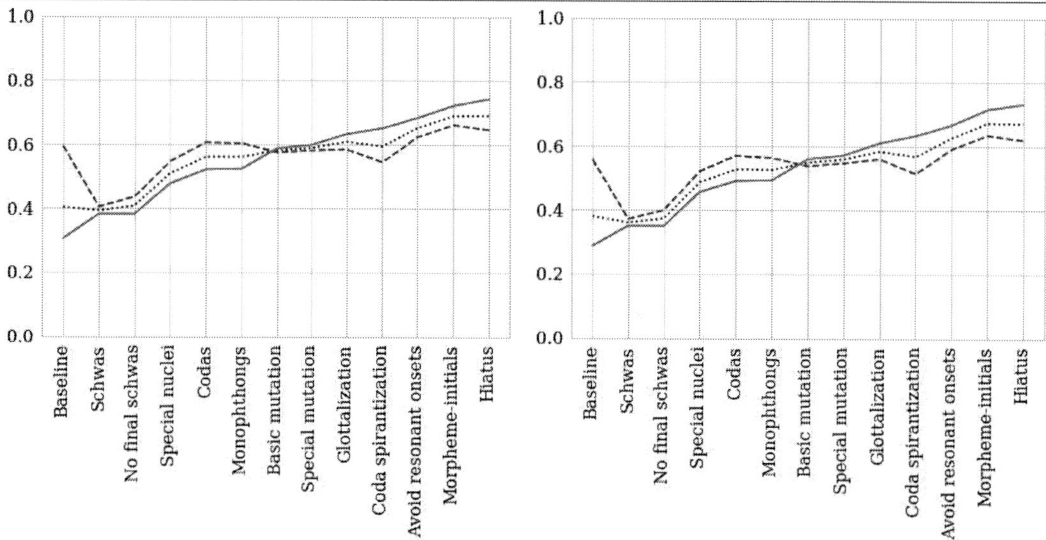

Figure 6: Improvements to recall (red solid line), precision (purple dashed line), and F1 (black dotted line) on the development (left) and test (right) documents by the implementation of specific phonological rules and constraints.

of suffixes can and cannot be dropped). We did not, however, fix any errors during the course of this experiment, so that score improvement would reflect only development effort, not re-annotation.

The remaining errors, however, suggest there are still some missing aspects of our understanding of Kwak'wala morphophonology (e.g., exactly when [ə] or [a] is inserted at morpheme boundaries) or that some of the assumptions that we had made when proposing underlying forms may be too strict (e.g. the assumption that there are only three underlying vowels). These are things we had previously suspected, but the development of an explicit computational system such as this helps to identify (and perhaps even quantify) those parts of Kwak'wala phonology and morphophonology for which our understanding is incomplete.

7 Further development

As continued development unearths an increasing percentage of errors and idiosyncrasies in the corpus itself, it may be beneficial in further development to switch to a new corpus, so that additional rules/-constraints are more likely to generalize to text by other authors, rather than overfit to our own style of transcription and analysis.

Also, this component is only one part of the intended OCR pipeline, which will also require:

- An OCR model to extract texts in historical orthographies. Fortuitously, Hubert et al. (2016) has already trained a model to recognize historical text in Haida that used the same font and almost all the same diacritics.

- A conversion system between the historical orthography and modern orthographies. Such a system already exists at `orth.nfshost.com`, however it implements a one-to-one correspondence that would be inappropriate for this task. A many-to-many orthographic transducer may, however, be adapted using its conversion tables as a starting point.

- A morphological component specifying the known roots, suffixes, and enclitics of Kwak'wala, as well as the possible arrangements of these.

These three components, along with the phonological component here, should help to correct and normalize errors in the recognition of historical texts, and thus help make the Boas corpus more accessible to modern readers and researchers.

Acknowledgments

This research would not have been possible without my consultants' patient instruction and their many years of effort in sharing their language. Data collection was supported by the Jacobs Research Funds. Any errors or misconceptions are my own.

References

Stephen R. Anderson. 1985. Typological distinctions in word formation. In Timothy Shopen, editor, *Language Typology and Syntactic Description, Volume III: Grammatical Categories in the Lexicon*, pages 1–65. Cambridge University Press, Cambridge, UK.

Mark Baker. 1996. *The Polysynthesis Parameter*. Oxford University Press, Oxford.

Kenneth R. Beesley and Lauri Karttunen. 2003. *Finite State Morphology*. CSLI Publications.

Franz Boas and George Hunt. 1902. Kwakiutl texts. *Memoirs of the American Museum of Natural History*, 5.

Franz Boas, Helene Boas Yampolsky, and Zellig S Harris. 1947. Kwakiutl grammar with a glossary of the suffixes. *Transactions of the American Philosophical Society, New Series*, 37(3):203–377, Dec.

FirstVoices. 2009. Kwak'wala: Words. Retrieved from http://www.firstvoices.com/en/Kwakwala/words on Oct. 22, 2014.

Isabell Hubert, Antti Arppe, Jordan Lachler, and Eddie Antonio Santos. 2016. Training & quality assessment of an optical character recognition model for Northern Haida. In Nicoletta Calzolari (Conference Chair), Khalid Choukri, Thierry Declerck, Sara Goggi, Marko Grobelnik, Bente Maegaard, Joseph Mariani, Helene Mazo, Asuncion Moreno, Jan Odijk, and Stelios Piperidis, editors, *Proceedings of the Tenth International Conference on Language Resources and Evaluation (LREC 2016)*, Paris, France, May. European Language Resources Association (ELRA).

Mans Hulden. 2009. Foma: a finite-state compiler and library. In *Proceedings of the 12th Conference of the European Chapter of the Association for Computational Linguistics*, pages 29–32. Association for Computational Linguistics.

Lauri Karttunen. 1998. The proper treatment of optimality theory in computational linguistics. In Lauri Karttunen and Kemal Oflazer, editors, *Proceedings of the International Workshop on Finite State Methods in Natural Language Processing (FSMNLP)*.

Donald Knuth. 1992. *Literate Programming*. California: Stanford University Center for the Study of Language and Information.

Neville J. Lincoln and John C. Rath. 1980. *North Wakashan Comparative Root List*. National Museums of Canada, Ottawa, ON.

Neville J. Lincoln and John C. Rath. 1986. *Phonology, dictionary and listing of roots and lexical derivates of the Haisla language of Kitlope and Kitimaat, B.C.* National Museums of Canada, Ottawa, ON.

Patrick Littell. 2016. *Focus, Predication, and Polarity in Kwak'wala*. Ph.D. thesis, University of British Columbia.

Mike Maxwell and Jonathan D. Amith. 2005. Language documentation: The Nahuatl grammar. In Alexander Gelbukh, editor, *Computational Linguistics and Intelligent Text Processing*, pages 474–485, Berlin, Heidelberg. Springer Berlin Heidelberg.

Mike Maxwell. 2012. Electronic grammars and reproducible research. In Sebastian Nordoff, editor, *Electronic Grammaticography*, pages 207–235, Honolulu. University of Hawaii Press.

Alan Prince and Paul Smolensky. 1993. *Optimality Theory: Constraint Interaction in Generative Grammar*. Technical Report, Rutgers University Center for Cognitive Science and Computer Science Department, University of Colorado at Boulder.

Caro Struijke. 1998. Reduplicant and output TETU in Kwakwala. In H. Fukazawa, F. Morelli, C. Struijke, and Y. Su, editors, *University of Maryland Working Papers, Vol. 7: Papers in Phonology*, pages 150–178. University of Maryland Working Papers.

Caro Struijke. 2000. *Existential Faithfulness: A Study of Reduplicative TETU, Feature Movement, and Dissimilation*. Ph.D. thesis, University of Maryland.

A prototype finite-state morphological analyser for Chukchi

Vasilisa Andriyanets
School of Linguistics
Higher School of Economics
Moscow
bandrandr@yandex.ru

Francis M. Tyers
School of Linguistics
Higher School of Economics
Moscow
ftyers@hse.ru

Abstract

In this article we describe the application of finite-state transducers to the morphological and phonological systems of Chukchi, a polysynthetic language spoken in the north of the Russian Federation. The language exhibits progressive and regressive vowel harmony, productive incorporation and extensive circumfixing. To implement the analyser we use the well-known Helsinki Finite-State Toolkit (HFST). The resulting model covers the majority of the morphological and phonological processes. A brief evaluation carried out on publically-available corpora shows that the coverage of the transducer is between and 53% and 76%. An error evaluation of 100 tokens randomly selected from the corpus, which were not covered by the analyser shows that most of the morphological processes are covered and that the majority of errors are caused by a limited stem lexicon.

1 Introduction

This paper describes a new morphological analyser for Chukchi, an endangered language spoken on the Chukotka Peninsula in north of the Russian Federation (see Figure). The analyser is based on finite-state technology, which means that it can be used for both the analysis and the generation of forms — a finite-state morphological transducer maps between surface forms and lexical forms (lemmas and morphosyntactic tags).

An analyser of this sort has a wide variety of uses, including for automating the process of corpus annotation for linguistic research as well as for creating proofing tools (such as spellcheckers) and for lemmatising for electronic dictionary lookup for language learners — in a language with heavy prefixing and suffixing morphology, determining the stem is not a simple matter.

Our approach is based on the Helsinki Finite-State Toolkit (HFST, Linden et al. (2011)). We chose this toolkit over other toolkits such as `foma` Hulden (2009), as in addition to the `xfst` sequential rule formalism it also supports two-level phonological rules and weighted automata. We took an existing machine-readable dictionary and converted it to the `lexc` lexicon format, we then implemented the morphotactics (morpheme combinatorics) in `lexc` and used two-level (`twol`) rules for modelling phonological and some morphotactic constraints.

The remainder of the paper is laid out as follows: Section 2 gives a short introduction to Chukchi from a grammatical and sociolinguistic perspective; Section 3 describes other attempts at building a morphological analyser for Chukchi; Section 4 describes the methodology we used when building the transducer, including the tools used ; Section 5 describes in more detail what has been done and what problems arose when building the analyser; Section 6 describes a small evaluation and finally Section 7 contains our plans for future work.

2 Chukchi

Chukchi (in Chukchi: *дыгъоравэтльэн йиԓыйиԓ* /ɬəɣʔorawetɬʔen jiɬəjiɬ/, ISO 639-3: `ckt`) is a highly-endangered minority language of the Russian Federation. It is spoken by around 5,000 people across the Chukotka Peninsula. Like the vast majority of other languages of the Russian Federation, intergenerational transmission is breaking down and there are few children learning the language. There are several relatively

Proceedings of Workshop on Polysynthetic Languages, pages 31–40
Santa Fe, New Mexico, USA, August 20-26, 2018.

Figure 1: Location of Chukchi-speaking area within the Russian Federation

similar spoken dialects and a written standard variety, which has been codified in a Soviet-era reference grammar, (Skorik, 1977) and differs from colloquial varities in a number of ways. The work described in this article is largely based on Dunn (1999). Dunn's grammar is written mostly for the Telqep dialect, which is spoken in the Tawajwaam village close to Anadyr, the administrative centre of Chukotka.

Chukchi is an ergative–absolutive language with rich morphology, both inflectional and derivational. In the nominal inflectional paradigm there are 13 cases and two numbers and in the verbal inflectional paradigm there are hundreds of forms. The language exhibits vowel harmony. Vowel harmony is a linguistic phenomenon where vowels are grouped and only vowels from the same group can occur in one word (cf. in most of the Turkic languages and some of the Uralic languages). That means, (almost) all vowels in a word can change if a certain affix is attached. The exact domain of vowel harmony can differ depending on the language.

In Chukchi vowels are split into two groups based on vowel height plus the schwa, which is neutral. Vowels in the first group, *э, o, a* /e$_2$, o, a/, are referred to as dominant, while vowels in the second group, *и, y, э* /i, u, e$_1$/ are referred to as recessive. Note that the difference between /e$_1$/ and /e$_2$/ is only a matter of harmony, they are pronounced the same. What is more, vowel harmony in Chukchi, unlike Turkic or Uralic languages, works both progressively and regressively and applies over the whole word. That is, morphological and phonological features of a suffix can cause vowel changes in the stem or vice versa — over any part of the phonological word. For example, a word *дылекэли* /ɬəɬekeɬi/ 'spectacled eider'[1] has recessive vowels, so if the dominant vowel harmony ablative case suffix *-гыпы* /ɣəpə/ is attached, the final form would be *дылякалэгыпы* /ɬəɬaka**ɬ**eɣəpə/ 'from the spectacled eider' where harmonised vowels are indicated in bold. As can be seen in this example, the vowel *э* has both dominant and regressive readings and is both a dominant pair to /i/ and a regressive pair to /a/. This was one of the challenges for us while composing the transducer.

This is illustrated with some further examples. In example (1) the vowels in the stem *дылекэли* which are recessive are harmonised to the dominant variant after the addition of the ablative suffix *-гыпы* /ɣəpə/, which does not contain any dominant vowels (the two vowels are schwas), but in any case causes dominant harmony. Then in example (2), the essive case suffix vowel *-y* /u/ is harmonised to the dominant form *-o* /o/ after being attached to the stem *айван* /ajwan/ 'Eskimo' which has dominant vowels. Finally, in Example (3), the vowels in the stem *ээк-* /eek/ 'lamp' are harmonised to their dominant forms after the addition of the derivational suffix *-аукача-* /aŋqatça/ 'side'.

	Recessive	Д	Ы	Л	е	К	э	Л	и	+	Г	Ы	П	Ы	= дылекэли- + -гыпы
(1)					↓		↓		↓						
	Dominant	Д	Ы	Л	я	К	а	Л	э	+	Г	Ы	П	Ы	= дылякалэгыпы

	Recessive	а	й	в	а	н	+	у	= айван- + -y
(2)								↓	
	Dominant	а	й	в	а	н	+	о	= айвано

---

[1]Lat. *somateria fischeri*, a large sea duck found in northeastern Siberia.

32

Agreement	Non-future	Example		Translation
1 Sg	т- **stem** -(гъэ)-к	*тэквэтгъэк*	/tekwetɣʔek/	'I leave'
1 Pl	мыт- **stem** -мык	*мытэквэтмык*	/mətekwetmək/	'We leave'
2 Sg	**stem** -(гъ)-и	*эквэтгъи*	/ekwetɣʔi/	'You leave'
2 Pl	**stem** -тык	*эквэттык*	/ekwettək/	'You leave'
3 Sg	**stem** -(гъ)-и	*эквэтгъи*	/ekwetɣʔi/	'She leaves'
3 Pl	**stem** -(гъэ)-т	*эквэтгъэт*	/ekwetɣʔet/	'They leave'

Table 1: Conjugation of intransitive verbs in the non-future/aorist tense, the verb has agreement markers for S, which denotes the syntactic role of a single-argument intransitive verb. Note the circumfix for the first person plural. Parentheses indicate optionality. Examples are based on the stem *-эквэт-* /ekwet/ 'leave'.

		O					
		1 Sg	1 Pl	2 Sg	2 Pl	3 Sg	3 Pl
A	1 Sg	—	—	т- **stem** -гыт	т- **stem** -тык	т- **stem** -(гъэ)-н	т- **stem** -нэт
	1 Pl	—	—	мыт- **stem** -гыт	мыт- **stem** -тык	мыт- **stem** -(гъэ)-н	мыт- **stem** -нэт
	2 Sg	инэ- **stem** -(гъ)-и	**stem** -тку-гъ-и	—	—	**stem** -(гъэ)-н	**stem** -нэт
	2 Pl	инэ- **stem** -тык	**stem** -тку-тык	—	—	**stem** -ткы	
	3 Sg	инэ- **stem** -(гъ)-и	нэ- **stem** -мык	нэ- **stem** -гыт	нэ- **stem** -тык	**stem** -нин	**stem** -ннпэт
	3 Pl	нэ- **stem** -гым				нэ- **stem** -(гъэ)-н	нэ- **stem** -нэт

Table 2: Conjugation of transitive verbs for agreement in the non-future/aorist tense. A is the semantic agent, or something that acts analogously and O is the semantic patient or anything else that acts analogously. For example, if we take the stem *-ɟьу-* /ʔʔu/ 'see' and we add the agreement morphemes *мыт-* /mət/ and *-гыт* /ɣət/ we get the form *мытɟьугыт* /mətʔuɣət/ 'We see you'. Empty cells show impossible agreement combinations and parentheses indicate optionality. The table is adapted from (Dunn, 1999, p.177).

$$
(3) \quad
\begin{array}{l}
\text{Recessive} \quad \text{э} \;\; \text{э} \;\; \text{к} \;+\; \text{а} \;\; \text{ӈ} \;\; \text{ӄ} \;\; \text{а} \;\; \text{ч} \;\; \text{а} \;+\; \text{г} \;\; \text{т} \;\; \text{ы} \;=\; \text{ээк- + -аӈӄача- + -гты} \\
\qquad\qquad\quad\;\; \downarrow \;\; \downarrow \\
\text{Dominant} \quad \text{а} \;\; \text{а} \;\; \text{к} \;+\; \text{а} \;\; \text{ӈ} \;\; \text{ӄ} \;\; \text{а} \;\; \text{ч} \;\; \text{а} \;+\; \text{г} \;\; \text{т} \;\; \text{ы} \;=\; \text{аакаӈӄачагты}
\end{array}
$$

Chukchi also has many morphophonological processes, which are expressed via mutations of letters in some contexts. This is further complicated by standard Chukchi orthography, which in some cases does not reflect the order of the sounds in a consistent manner.[2] For example, the glottal stop before a vowel at the beginning of a word or between two vowels is written as an apostrophe ' sign *after* the (second) vowel, while it is written as ъ or ь in other positions. Thus, the word *a'тчак* /ʔattɕak/ 'to wait' actually starts with the glottal stop when pronounced. This is further complicated by the fact that when prefixed, the glottal stop becomes a ь or ъ sign *before* the vowel, e.g. the neutral aspect aorist (non-future), first person singular agent, second person singular object form of *a'тчак* /ʔattɕak/ would be *мытъатчагыт* /mətʔattɕaɣət/ 'I wait for you'. Figures 1 and 2 show an example table from Dunn (1999) for neutral aspect aorist for transitive and intransitive verbs respectively.

In terms of morphology, Chukchi inflectional morphology is both suffixing and prefixing, and in many cases circumfixing. Chukchi transitive verbs have A–O agreement and inflect for both subject and object,[3] but the combinations are not agglutinative and cannot be divided into "affixes for A" and "affixes for O".

Chukchi derivational morphology is abundant and very productive, with both derivational prefixes, such as *рэ-* /re/ for desiderative and suffixes such as *-тку* /tku/ for iterative.

3 Related work

There was an attempt at making a morphological analyser for Chukchi verbs and nouns using Uniparser (Arkhangelsky, 2012). This used an approach to morphological analysis based on affix stripping with surface

---

[2]Our rationale behind building the transducer based on the official orthography is that we would like to have the possibility of producing a proofing tool, and the ease of treating Russian loanwords — which would be complicated by transcription.

[3]Here we follow the terminology of Dunn (1999) in labelling the subject of an intransitive verb as S, or 'subject' and the subject of a transitive verb as A or 'agent'. Dunn (1999) defines S as "…the syntactic role of the single argument denoted by the syntactic valency of an intransitive verb" and states that "…A and O are distinguished from S in that they are with reference to the syntactic valency of a transitive verb".

constraints using regular expressions (no underlying forms). While the system was able to analyse some part of the Chukchi noun paradigm, it was not able to deal with circumfixes, incorporation or long-distance morphological dependencies. We used the machine-readable lexicon to bootstrap our lexc lexicon.

4 Methdology

The transducer described in this paper is designed based on the Helsinki Finite State Toolkit (HFST, (Linden et al., 2011)), which is popular in the field of morphological analysis. It implements both the lexc formalism for defining lexicon and morphotactics, and the twol and xfst formalisms for modelling morphophonological rules. This toolkit has been chosen because it, or the related foma (Hulden, 2009), has been widely used for other agglutinative and polysynthetic languages, such as Navajo (Hulden and Bischoff, 2008), the Dene languages (Arppe et al., 2017), Quechua (Rios, 2016) and Arapaho (Kazeminejad et al., 2017), and is available under a free/open-source licence.

A finite-state transducer is a formal way to map surface forms and analyses (lexical forms) to one another. For example, *гэӈээккэтэ* /ɣeŋeekkete/ 'сом-daughter-сом' would receive the analysis нээккэт<n><com>.[4]

The transducer accepts the form as input and outputs the analysis, and vice versa. When used for modelling natural-language morphology, a finite-state transducer is a directed graph where the arcs encode relations between input symbols and output symbols. These symbols may be letters, linguistic tags or archiphonemes[5] Analysing or generating a form involves traversing the graph from left to right, while reading a symbol and outputting its corresponding symbol.

5 Implementation

The full transducer is composed of three transducers:

- lexc deals with morphology and lexicon;

- twoc helps to implement morphology that is not possible (or too difficult) to implement in lexc, e.g. certain circumfixes;

- twol deals with phonology and morphophonology.

In the following subsections we describe each of these components in turn.

5.1 Lexc

The dictionary we took roots from consisted of 6,321 lexemes, divided into 10 word classes. The resulting lexc file contains 15 continuation classes for nouns, one continuation class for verbs that led to either transitive or intransitive class, and several other classes to cover closed classes such as pronouns and conjunctions.

One of the drawbacks of the dictionary we used was that it did not include information on the transitivity of verbs — this causes a problem because transitive and intransitive verbs inflect very differently (see Tables 1 and 2). This meant that we had to guess the transitivity of a verb by its affixes. This kind of guessing is possible for finite forms (as the agreement suffixes differ between transitive and intransitive), but increases the size of the transducer and is impossible for non-finite forms (as they are not marked for agreement in the same way). As the transitivity of a verb form is fairly clear from the affixes, given a large enough corpus it should be possible to semi-automatically determine the transitivity of individual stems, however any guesses made this way would need to be proofread.

Not having the verbs marked for transitivity can cause two problems, the first being that we may analyse forms that do not exist (for example, an intransitive suffix on a transitive verb stem); the second being that these combinations may be homographous with word forms that do exist, resulting in an incorrect analysis and potential for *hiding* gaps in the lexicon.

To include circumfixes in the analysis, flag diacritics were used. This allowed the output tags for words with circumfixes to follow the Apertium (Forcada et al., 2011) tag style. Flag diacritics are a

---

[4]The tags used here mean 'noun' and 'comitative case'. See appendix 5 for a list of the tags used in this article.

[5]An archiphoneme is a symbol represents an underspecified phoneme which is determined by context; that is a phoneme which can have more than one surface realisation depending on context.

way of restricting certain combinations of discontinuous parts of words. They have the format @FLAG-TYPE.FEATURE.VALUE@, where FLAGTYPE is the type of the flag, i.e. what it does: whether it sets the value of a feature (P flags), requires certain value of a feature (R flags) or demands that a feature has not been given value at all (D flags); FEATURE is the name of the feature one gives, and VALUE is the value of the feature that should or should not be matched with other flag diacritics with the same FEATURE or other FLAGTYPEs. For example, the verbal prefix used in the intransitive <s_sg1> form *мыт-* /mɔt/ sets the value of a feature VPR (verbal prefix) to myt: @P.VPR.myt@. Then, after the root, the suffix part of the <s_sg1> circumfix demands the value of the feature VPR to be set to myt: @R.VPR.myt@. Other suffixes demand either other prefixes or that the value of the feature is not set: @D.VPR@.

The tag style we used was that the lemma always preceded the tags, and the order of the tags was the following: first the category tags (like <v>); prefix derivations; suffix derivations; inflection. This posed a certain challenge for us and basically required treating every prefix in the same manner as a circumfix, as the morpheme appeared before the stem, but the tag appeared after stem. The system presented in Kazeminejad et al. (2017), where tags appear *in situ*, which could lead to a more efficient implementation, but less uniform tag strings. We made that choice based on considerations of tagset simplicity as opposed to implementation simplicity.

It was decided that all of the verbal inflection paradigm should be written with flag diacritics, as every inflected verb has some of the inflection affixes, and flag diacritics cut the number of branches in the resulting transducer down, making the transducer smaller. Some parts of prefixal and circumfixal verbal derivation, however, were moved to the twoc module, as the overflow of flag diacritics would make the source files unreadable.

5.2 Twoc

The twoc module included twolc-style rules for prefixes. The purpose of these rules was to be able to have the tag representing the feature to appear later in the string than where the morpheme appeared. For example, consider the form *қинэнимэтги* /qinenimetgi/ '(You) make me curdle!', which has the underlying form: ҟ{ы}>ин{Æ}>{R}{ы}>им{Æ}т>и (glossed: INTL.ASG2.OSG1.CAUS-curdle-ASG2.OSG1). In order to get the causative tag to appear after the stem we add markers in the tag string, enclosed in square brackets at the point at where the morpheme appears and at the point at which the tag appears,

Surface form:	ҟинэнимэтги
Morphotactic form:	ҟ{ы}>ин{Æ}>{R}{ы}>им{Æ}т>и
Lexical form:	[+caus]имэтык<v><tv>[+caus]<caus><neut><intn><a_sg2><o_sg1>

We then introduce a twol rule (see following) which forbids strings where only a single [+caus] marker appears (e.g. the prefix without the tag, or the tag without the prefix).

```
"Causative"
%[%+caus%]:0 <=>          _ :* %[%+caus%]:0 ;
        %[%+caus%]:0 :* _ ;
```

The difference between these rules and the flag diacritics mentioned previously is that they do not require processing at runtime.

5.3 Twol

The twol part of the transducer treated orthographic, phonologic and morphophonologic rules. In twol each rule is compiled into a transducer and all the rules are applied simultaneously.[6]

Two-level rules are equivalent in expressive power to sequential rules (Karttunen, 1993), however from the point of view of the linguist they have some differences particularly in how phonology is conceptualised.

---

[6]A reviewer suggests that xfst-style sequential rules are the dominant paradigm for implementing morphophonological rules. We would dispute this, while sequential rules are definitely popular, two large repositories of freely-available morphological transducers, Apertium (Forcada et al., 2011) and Giellatekno (Moshagen et al., 2014) are largely based on two-level rules, with Apertium having none out of 77 transducers based on sequential rules and Giellatekno having six out of 52.

```
"Vowel harmony"
! а й в а н >:0 у:о
Vx:Vy <=> [ Dominant | %{+VH%}: ] :* _ ;
                               _ :* [ Dominant | %{+VH%}: ] ;
       except
                         .#. _ %>: :Vow ;               ! contexts for deletion
                        :Cns _ (:0) (:0) %>: :Vow ;     ! deletion; (:0) (:0) = special symbols
                           _ :*   %>: %{ә%}: ;          ! doesn't affect loan phonology
                           _ %{°%}:0 .#. ;              ! word-final abs reduction
                           _ %{·%}:0 .#. ;              ! word-final abs deletion
        [ :ч | :□ ] (:0) (:0) _ ;                       ! orthography
:Vow (:0) (:0) й: (:0) (:0) _ ;                         ! orthography
       where
           Vx in ( у ю и %{Æ%} )
           Vy in ( о ё э   а   ) matched ;
```

Figure 2: A twol rule to apply vowel harmony constraints. A vowel Vx is changed to Vy if there is any dominant vowel anywhere in the string, or if the special marker of dominant harmony {+VH} appears. The except contexts apply to loanwords, vowels which are deleted, and vowels which are processed by other rules because of orthographic rules, e.g. *u* /i/ should change to *e* /e/ and not э /e/ in certain contexts.

In two-level rules, the rules are viewed as constraints over a set of all possible surface forms generated by expanding the underlying forms using the alphabet, whereas in sequential rules, the rules are viewed as a sequence of operations for converting an underlying to a surface form. While it may not be relevant from an engineering point of view, we find conceiving of rules as constraints over all possible forms to be more cognitively plausible. Readers are encouraged to review Karttunen (1993) for a more thorough comparison of the techniques.

The most important set of rules was for vowel harmony. This involved dealing with both phonological considerations and orthographic considerations. First of all, all of the vowels in the word should agree for harmony class. Second, after the letter *ӡ* /ɬ/ in the Cyrillic orthography vowels are written with Russian iotated vowels, so that the sequences *ӡe* /ɬe/ and *нэ* /ne/ have the same vowel. Finally, Russian loanwords can contain otherwise impossible combinations of vowels and always behave as if they were dominant, i.e. they do not change. For example, in the word *округ*[7] there are two vowels (*o* /o/ and *y* /u/) which form a harmonic pair: *o* /o/ is dominant, while *y* /u/ is recessive, i.e. it usually changes in the presence of a dominant vowel or a dominant harmony marker. A special sign ({Ӕ}) was introduced so as to not overwrite the vowels in such cases. The general-case vowel harmony rule is given in Figure 2. This rule turns vowels listed in the where section in the end as Vx to vowels listed there as Vy in certain contexts.

There is also a set of rules that govern syllable structure. Chukchi has a strict syllable structure: the maximal structure is CVC, usually CV. On one hand, if a consonant cluster of three or more consonants occurs, it is syllabified with a schwa, *ы* in the orthography. If multiple contexts co-occur, CV(C) syllable templates are assigned to sounds from right to left, and then schwas are inserted. An illustration of this process can be seen in Figure 3.

On the other hand, the onsets of syllables are always filled (unless the word starts with a vowel), so if two or more vowels occur next to each other, the first one is deleted.

Other phonological processes that were dealt with were vowel deletion, consonant deletion in certain contexts, affix allomorphy, vowel reduction, and archiphonemic allomorphy.

5.4 Results

The Figure 4 below shows the example output from the transducer.

So far, the analyser accounts for:

- the vast majority of morphophonology and orthography issues;

- nominal, pronominal, adjectival inflection and derivation; uninflected parts of speech;

---

[7]Rus. /бкруг/, an administrative division often translated as 'district'.

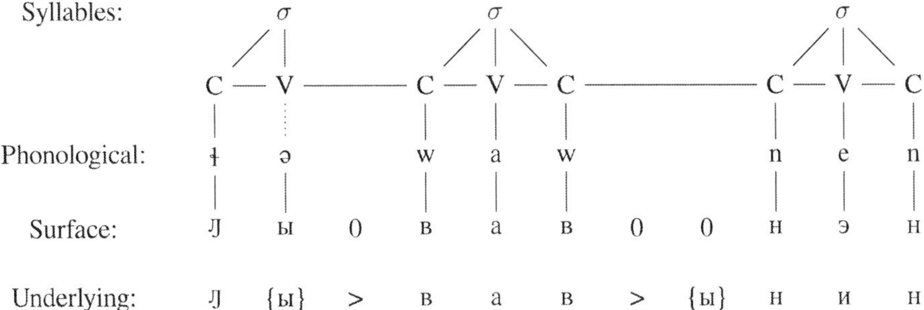

Figure 3: Process of syllabification, note that a schwa is inserted to avoid an impossible syllabic sequence *ɟвав- /ʜwaw-/*. Possible schwa positions are included in the `lexc` morphotactic structure using the archiphoneme {ы}. Note how in the example the first {ы} appears as ы on the surface while the second one appears as 0, effectively being deleted. The change from $u \to ə$ is as a result of the vowel harmony rule, see Figure 2.

Corpus	Tokens	Coverage	Mean ambiguity
Fairy tales (1)	26,109	76.6	1.43
Fairy tales (2)	45,654	62.2	–
Fiction (1)	29,148	58.8	–
Fiction (2)	23,352	53.1	–
Periodicals	38,552	53.7	–
Total:	162,815	60.9	1.43

Table 3: Coverage of the analyser over a range of publically-available corpora.

- verbal inflection (except for certain future paradigm cells);

- verbal derivation.

It also contains structures to parse compounds and incorporation, but turning these on causes the transducer to explode in size to the point of being uncompilable due to lack of memory. We suspect that this has to do with how we use `twol` to enforce tag placement, and intend to solve this problem going forward (see Section 7).

6 Evaluation

We performed a short evaluation on the results of the analyser for lexical coverage and also an error analysis of unknown tokens.

6.1 Coverage

The naïve coverage and mean ambiguity of the morphological analyser were determined. Naïve coverage is the percentage of surface forms in a given corpora that receive at least one morphological analysis. Forms counted by this measure may have other analyses which are not delivered by the transducer. The mean ambiguity measure was calculated as the average number of analyses returned per token in the corpus.

6.2 Error analysis

In order to determine the completeness of the implementation we performed a limited error analysis of tokens in our corpus which received no analysis from the transducer. We selected 100 forms at random and classified them into the following error classes: missing stem, incorporation, missing morphotactics, compounding, missing phonology, and typographical error.

As can be seen in Table 4 the vast majority of errors are caused by an incomplete lexicon. This is fortunately the easiest part to improve.

Surface form	Analyses
Аӈқачормык	аӈқачормын<n><loc>
	аӈқы<n><side><loc>
ырытқэй	ырыт<n><dim><sg><abs>
тэйкынин	тэйкык<v><tv><neut><aor><a_sg3><o_sg3>
,	,<cm>
ымы	ымы<adv>
	ымы<cnjadv>
рыннокон	рыннокон<n><px3sg><abs>
	рыннокон<n><sg><abs>
тэйкынин	тэйкык<v><tv><neut><aor><a_sg3><o_sg3>
,	,<cm>
лыгэн	лыгэн<part>
тэйкып丁ыткунэӈу	тэйкык<v><iv><compl><ger><ess>
	тэйкык<v><iv><compl><gna_res>
	тэйкык<v><tv><compl><ger><ess>
рырыткувнин	*рырыткувнин
.	.<sent>

Figure 4: Example of output from the analyser for the sentence *Аӈқачормык ырытқэй тэйкынин, ымы рыннокон тэйкынин лыгэн тэйкып丁ыткунэӈу рырыткувнин* 'By the coast he made a little bow, he made an arrow, just after finishing making them he broke them.' An asterisk marks a word unknown to the analyser.

Category	Frequency	Percentage (%)
Missing stem	82	75.2
Missing morphotactics	15	13.7
Incorporation	7	6.4
Missing phonology	2	1.8
Typographical error	3	2.7
Total:	109	100

Table 4: Proportion of errors by category. Note that although there were only 100 words selected, the number of errors adds up to more than 100 as some words evinced more than one kind of error.

The two words which were categorised for phonological error were *уққэм-қэй* 'bowl-DIM' and *пыкиры-丁ьы-н* 'arrive-PTCP-SG.ABS'. The problem with the first one was that the stem is actually *уққэмэ* and there is a process of final vowel deletion in absolutive, but this process should not happen with derivations. The problem with the second one was that the schwas behave differently with glottal stops: in some cases a glottal stop is counted as a consonant in the stem structure and therefore the schwa is inserted while in other cases the glottal stop is not a consonant, and the schwa does not get inserted. We chose the last strategy as it seemed to be more frequent. Treating this going forward may involve including rules to deal with irregularities.

Multiple words lack stems, but we can guess the form and what the stem looks like, for example, *ы'ны-ргы-тку-н* is clearly a verb with its subject in third plural and its object in third singular with an iterative derivation, like 'A3PL-**stem**-ITER-O3SG'.

An example of missing morphotactics is *нэт丁е-қэй*, which can be glossed as 'soon-DIM', although in our transducers there is no diminutive derivation for adverbs.

Typographical errors could be exemplified by *тыт丁епы* 'open a door', a word that exists in our dictionaries as *тыт丁ёпы*, with *ё* instead of *е* (this is a common misplacement with Cyrillic alphabet).

An example of a wordform that caused both an 'incorporation error' and a 'missing stem error' is *ты-мэмы丁-енаванҷаты-п丁ытко-гъа-к*, which lacks a known stem, but can be glossed as 's1SG-seal-**stem-**

COMPL-TH-s1SG', with a completive derivational suffix and a thematic inflectional element. The word 'seal'
is clearly incorporated in a verbal form.

7 Future work

As can be seen from the error analysis, the most pressing concern is to expand the lexicon. Unfortunately
there are no other machine-readable published dictionaries of Chukchi, so to a certain extent this would
need to be done by hand. One possible approach would be to use a guesser module which could guess the
tags for unknown roots and then check them manually.

We are also planning to come up with a solution for incorporation and compounding and are currently
investigating possible approaches.

A third idea is to look at reworking some of the phonological processes. Either by splitting all of the processes into separate rules by switching to rewrite rules, as in e.g. Chen and Schwartz (2018), or alternatively
having several levels of two-level rules, e.g. splitting the application of schwa epenthesis (see Figure 3) into
a separate ruleset.

As this project is now cooperating with the research community working on Amguema dialect,[8] another
possible avenue for improvement would be to adapt the analyser to this variety of Chukchi.

In the longer term, we would like to investigate the creation of a spellchecker, although the coverage of the
lexicon is currently too small, the sparsity of corpus data and the complexity of Chukchi morphology make
finite-state spellchecking, such as described in Pirinen and Lindén (2014) a promising avenue. Making a
functional tool would also give the opportunity to engage with the Chukchi-speaking language community
itself, who have so far unfortunately not been directly involved in the development process.

In addition given the significant interaction between morphology and syntax in Chukchi, and the lack of
any existing treebanks for polysynthetic languages, a treebank would be an interesting idea to work on.

8 Concluding remarks

We have presented the first finite-state morphological analyser for Chukchi, and the first computational
analyser which can treat a large part of its verbal morphology. The analyser is free and open-source, meaning
that it can be used and extended by anyone interested.[9]

Acknowledgements

We are deeply grateful to Michael Dunn and Maria Pupynina for their help in the early stages of the project
and to the anonymous reviewers for their extensive and useful comments. The article was prepared within
the framework of the Academic Fund Programme at the National Research University Higher School of
Economics (HSE) in 2016 — 2018 (grant №17-05-0043) and by the Russian Academic Excellence Project
«5-100». It was also supported through the 2017 Google Summer of Code.

A Tagset

References

Arkhangelsky, T. (2012). *Принципы Построения Морфологического Парсера Для
Разноструктурных Языков.* PhD thesis, Lomonosov Moscow State University.

Arppe, A., Cox, C., Hulden, M., Lachler, J., Moshagen, S. N., Silfverberg, M., and Trosterud, T. (2017).
Computational modeling of the verb in Dene languages. The case of Tsuut'ina. In *Working Papers in
Athabascan Linguistics*, Red Book, pages 51–68. Alaska Native Language Center.

Chen, E. and Schwartz, L. (2018). A morphological analyzer for St. Lawrence Island / Central Siberian
Yupik. In *Proceedings of the 11th Language Resources and Evaluation Conference (LREC'18)*, Miyazaki,
Japan.

---

[8]More about this group can be found at `https://ling.hse.ru/chukchi/`

[9]The code, corpora and error analysis results described in this paper are available from GitHub at `https://github.com/BasilisAndr/chkchn` under a free/open-source licence.

Tag	Description	Tag	Description	Tag	Description	Tag	Description
<v>	Verb	<compl>	Completive	<tv>	Transitive	<side>	Derivation 'side'
<n>	Noun	<ptcp>	Participle	<iv>	Intransitive	<a_sg1>	A agreement SG1
<adj>	Adjective	<dem>	Demonstrative	<abs>	Absolutive	<a_sg2>	A agreement SG1
<adv>	Adverb	<dim>	Diminutive	<erg>	Ergative	<a_sg3>	A agreement SG1
<cnjadv>	Adverbial conjunction	<ger>	Gerund	<loc>	Locative	<o_sg1>	O agreement SG1
<cnjcoo>	Co-ordinating conjunction	<gna_res>	Resultative	<ess>	Essive	<o_sg3>	O agreement SG3
<post>	Postposition	<intn>	Intentional	<sg>	Singular	<o_pl2>	O agreement PL2
<prn>	Pronoun	<neut>	Neutral	<pl>	Plural	<o_pl3>	O agreement PL3
<ij>	Interjection	<pers>	Personal	<aor>	Aorist	<s_sg1>	S agreement SG1
<part>	Particle	<px3sg>	Possessive SG3	<caus>	Causative	<s_pl3>	S agreement PL3

Table 5: List of all tags used in the article.

Dunn, M. J. (1999). *A grammar of Chukchi*. PhD thesis, The Australian National University. `http://hdl.handle.net/1885/10769`.

Forcada, M. L., Ginestí-Rosell, M., Nordfalk, J., O'Regan, J., Ortiz-Rojas, S., Pérez-Ortiz, J. A., Sánchez-Martínez, F., Ramírez-Sánchez, G., and Tyers, F. M. (2011). Apertium: a free/open-source platform for rule-based machine translation. *Machine Translation*, 25(2):127–144.

Hulden, M. (2009). Foma: a finite-state compiler and library. In *Proceedings of the 12th Conference of the European Chapter of the Association for Computational Linguistics: Demonstrations Session*, pages 29–32. Association for Computational Linguistics.

Hulden, M. and Bischoff, S. T. (2008). An Experiment in Computational Parsing of the Navajo Verb. In Hulden, M. and Bischoff, S. T., editors, *Coyote Papers*, volume 16, pages 110–118. University of Arizona Linguistics Circle.

Karttunen, L. (1993). *The Last Phonological Rule: Reflections on constraints and derivations*, chapter Finite-state constraints. University of Chicago Press.

Kazeminejad, G., Cowell, A., and Hulden, M. (2017). Creating lexical resources for polysynthetic languages–the case of Arapaho. In *Proceedings of the 2nd Workshop on the Use of Computational Methods in the Study of Endangered Languages*, pages 10–18.

Linden, K., Silfverberg, M., Axelson, E., Hardwick, S., and Pirinen, T. (2011). *HFST–Framework for Compiling and Applying Morphologies*, volume 100 of *Communications in Computer and Information Science*, pages 67–85.

Moshagen, S., Trosterud, T., Rueter, J., Tyers, F. M., and Pirinen, T. A. (2014). Open-source infrastructures for collaborative work on under-resourced languages. In *Proceedings of CCURL workshop 2014 organised with LREC2014*.

Pirinen, T. A. and Lindén, K. (2014). State-of-the-art in weighted finite-state spell-checking. In *Proceedings of the 15th International Conference on Computational Linguistics and Intelligent Text Processing - Volume 8404*, CICLing 2014, pages 519–532, Berlin, Heidelberg. Springer-Verlag.

Rios, A. (2016). A basic language technology toolkit for Quechua. *Procesamiento del Lenguaje Natural*, (56):91–94.

Skorik, P. Y. (1977). *Грамматика чукотского языка: Глагол, наречие, служебные слова. Часть вторая*. Академия Наук СССР, Институт Языкознания.

Natural Language Generation for Polysynthetic Languages:
Language Teaching and Learning Software for Kanyen'kéha (Mohawk)

Greg Lessard
School of Computing
Queen's University
Canada
lessard@cs.queensu.ca

Nathan Brinklow
Department of Languages,
Literatures and Cultures
Queen's University
Canada
nathan.brinklow@queensu.ca

Michael Levison
School of Computing
Queen's University
Canada
levison@cs.queensu.ca

Abstract

Kanyen'kéha (in English, Mohawk) is an Iroquoian language spoken primarily in Eastern Canada (Ontario, Québec). Classified as endangered, it has only a small number of speakers and very few younger native speakers. Consequently, teachers and courses, teaching materials and software are urgently needed. In the case of software, the polysynthetic nature of Kanyen'kéha means that the number of possible combinations grows exponentially and soon surpasses attempts to capture variant forms by hand. It is in this context that we describe an attempt to produce language teaching materials based on a generative approach. A natural language generation environment (ivi/Vinci) embedded in a web environment (VinciLingua) makes it possible to produce, by rule, variant forms of indefinite complexity. These may be used as models to explore, or as materials to which learners respond. Generated materials may take the form of written text, oral utterances, or images; responses may be typed on a keyboard, gestural (using a mouse) or, to a limited extent, oral. The software also provides complex orthographic, morphological and syntactic analysis of learner productions. We describe the trajectory of development of materials for a suite of four courses on Kanyen'kéha, the first of which will be taught in the fall of 2018.

1 Background

Kanyen'kéha (in English, Mohawk) is one of the Iroquoian[1] languages, originally spoken in the area of what is now Ontario, Québec and New York. In the period after contact, a number of Mohawk groups left or were forced to leave their homelands in New York. Initial migrations to Québec were for political and religious reasons while later migrations were forced after the Mohawk allied themselves with the British during the Revolutionary War. The refugees were provided with lands in Upper Canada. Today, there are seven Kanyen'kehà:ka communities spread across Ontario, Québec and upper New York State.

Kanyen'kéha remained the dominant language of these communities into the 20th century. However, due to a variety of well documented factors, including government assimilation policy, the use of English education in day schools and residential schools, the proliferation and domination of English media, and the desire for parents to give their children a better life, the number of first language speakers declined significantly. This precipitous decline led Hoover (1992) to write: "It is not uncommon in Kahnawake to hear people conversing with their grandchildren in Mohawk, then switching to English to speak to their own children." In sum, Kanyen'kéha as a first language is arguably approaching the most severe level (8) on the Fishman scale (Fishman, 1991; Lewis and Simons, 2010). That is, almost all remaining L1 speakers are members of the grandparent generation, with perhaps a handful of young L1 bilinguals, the children of L2 speakers. It is difficult to determine precisely the number of remaining speakers of Kanyen'kéha, but current estimates put the number between 1000 and 1500.

Community leaders recognized the problem as it was developing and early language efforts began almost 50 years ago with night classes and the attempt to include the language in school curricula. Primary

---

[1]For an overview of the Iroquoian family, see Mithun (2006), and for more detail on the history of the Iroquoian languages, see Mithun (1984).

Proceedings of Workshop on Polysynthetic Languages, pages 41–52
Santa Fe, New Mexico, USA, August 20-26, 2018.

Immersion schools were started in many communities in the 1970's and 1980's. These were generally parent-led initiatives with community support that focused on cultural education in the language, but were not always long lasting or very effective in transmitting the language. In the 1990's, communities shifted their focus towards creating adult speakers through full-time adult immersion programs. These programs have met with success and continue to develop as they create speakers. The central role of second language learners is also recognized. According to Stacey (2016), "the future of Kanien'kéha will depend largely upon today's second-language speakers to become highly proficient speakers and pass the language on to their children". Similarly, Green (2017) argues for second language instruction embedded in an immersion framework. Or again, Hoover (1992) describes "two lines of attack: a series of Mohawk classes aimed at adult non-speakers of Mohawk, and a push for community insistence on the use of the Mohawk language whenever possible." However, these efforts are hampered by a lack of resources, including people, funding and teaching materials, as well as lack of opportunities to use the language outside the classroom.

2 Language teaching software: issues and desiderata

Along with other approaches, there have been attempts to produce language teaching software in Kanyen'kéha, including a version of Rosetta Stone (Bittinger, 2006), and a set of more advanced teaching materials including grammar exercises (Kanatawakhon-Maracle, 2002). Earlier still, collections of audio tapes, and later CD audio materials, were produced (Deering and Harries-Delisle, 2007). However, all these materials have been bedeviled by three factors.

One is the lack of academic grammars of the language, and of focussed studies of elements of the language. Many grammars are older (Bonvillain, 1973), as are many dictionaries (Bonvillain and Francis, 1972; Maracle, 2001; McDonald, 1977; Michelson, 1973). Most are not now distributed in any quantity. The same may be said of textbooks, which are relatively few and relatively difficult to obtain (Deering and Harries-Delisle, 2007; Kanatawakhon, 2013a; Kanatawakhon, 2013b).

Another factor is technological staleness: materials designed to be run on particular computer platforms become inaccessible when the platform disappears. Thus, the Rosetta Stone dataset, designed for an early version of the Rosetta software, is now not usable on more modern versions. This issue can be addressed to some degree by use of less 'physical' supports like websites, although web technologies also change over time (think of the disappearance of Flash).

A final, arguably more serious, factor stems from polysyntheticity itself. In the case of Kanyen'kéha, the verbal complex composed of the verb root plus a set of prefixed and suffixed forms may be extremely complex, as the following not unusual example illustrates:

(1) yaonsá:ke'

    y   *a*   *onsá:*   *k*   *e*   '
    there conditional future iterative me   to be somewhere punctual
    LOC TNS   IT   PRON V   ASP

    'I could go back there'

Here, elements of the verbal complex are separated by spaces, although in writing they would be joined. In addition, each of the elements shown here enters into a paradigmatic relation with other possible forms within the various classes, where LOC=locative, TNS=tense, IT=iterative, PRON=pronominal, V=verb, ASP=aspect. Thus, the translocative *ye* may be replaced by the cislocative *ti*, the *a* of the conditional future by *en* for the certain future. The iterative may appear as an alternate form with a different pronominal prefix. The resulting combinatorial explosion means that the set of possible combinations cannot reasonably be assembled by hand. As a result, much current language teaching software for polysynthetic languages focusses on simpler elements like greetings, nouns, names of objects and such, despite the clear need for more complex treatments (Kell, 2014; Montour, 2012).

One element of a solution to language teaching for polysynthetic languages lies, it has been argued, in the use of a generative approach. The question is, which one? We would argue that the response must take account of the diversity of expertise required to develop and maintain electronic teaching materials. This typically includes a) computer science, b) linguistics, c) knowledge of the language, and d) pedagogical expertise. Some of these areas of knowledge may be shared across individuals, but the fact remains that any system developed must be i) as easy as possible to program, maintain and extend in its component software, including adaptation to other dialects, and potentially other languages; ii) as linguistically transparent as possible in order to 'unbind' linguistic skills (i.e. grammar writing) from programming; iii) capable of capturing as many linguistic traits of a language as possible and producing written and oral output judged acceptable by speakers; iv) as media-rich as possible, including variations in input (text, audio, images) and output (typing, clicking, oral); and v) easily usable (and adaptable) by frontline language teachers to meet their needs, so that they become more than simply consumers of tools and materials produced by others.

3 Existing generative approaches

Current approaches to generating complex verbal materials for morphologically complex languages may be roughly divided into three categories: generation of materials from pre-existing corpus data, batch generative processing, and the use of Finite State Transducers.

3.1 Generation from corpus data

An example of this approach is provided by the Arikiturri system (Itziar Aldabe et al., 2006), used for teaching Basque, a morphologically rich language. The starting point is a corpus of morphologically and syntactically analyzed sentences, marked up in XML. The software combines these with specifications of areas of focus provided by language teachers to generate test questions, including fill-in-the-blank, word formation, multiple choice, and error correction. Along with questions and expected answers, the system generates distractors by making morphological changes to the expected answers. In addition, since Basque is a free word order language, the materials generated in each question may be reordered with respect to the original corpus materials. Evaluation of materials prior to use is provided in two ways: by an 'ill-formed sentence rejector' component in the system, and by an interface which permits a language teacher to select or reject candidate questions, as well as making some basic adjustments. Aldabe et al. argue that use of the system provides efficiencies compared to manual production of examples by teachers, but also note that there exist gaps in data provided by their corpus. This is unsurprising, given that even a very large corpus is unlikely to contain all possible forms. The difficulty is aggravated in the case of Canadian indigenous languages by the lack of tagged corpora of any reasonable size.

3.2 Batch generative processing

As an alternative to corpus-based construction of exercises, Perez Beltrachini et al. (2012) present a system called *GramEx*, based on Gardent et al. (2012), which uses Definite Clause Grammars representing the syntax and basic semantics of a language (in this case, French). These grammars are used to drive a Prolog query mechanism in order to produce a set of potential output sentences which are stored and may be queried to obtain sentences meeting desired patterns. These in turn are used to produce fill-in-the-blank and word order based exercises. Human intervention is still required, since the initial semantic specifications must be produced by hand, although a relatively small number of inputs produces a much larger set of outputs. In addition, a random sample of sentences produced by the grammar was evaluated by human experts. The system illustrates the power of a generative grammar, but the article provides few details on feedback provided to language learners, even for such primitive exercises as those presented. It is also unclear how the grammatical specifications used in the DCG for French could be adapted for Kanyen'kéha, where the potential number of inflected forms is significantly higher and where the placement of stress is context-dependent (see below). Finally, it is unclear how difficult it would be for a language teacher to add to or modify the system.

3.3 Use of Finite State Transducers

Arguably the most popular approach for dealing with morphologically rich languages is based on the use of Finite State Transducers, which may be described, in a nutshell, as rule-based devices for mapping between two sets of symbols such as, for example, an orthographic string as input and a morphological analysis as output, or vice-versa. For example in the Canadian context, FST's have been used to model nominal morphology (Snoek et al., 2014) and verb morphology (Harrigan et al., 2017) of Plains Cree, a polysynthetic language, and Harrigan et al. list a number of other similar projects. Harrigan notes as well that FST's can be applied to produce spellcheckers, paradigm generators, or components for CALL systems. Since our focus here is on CALL, we describe briefly three FST-based CALL systems, to illustrate their respective advantages and weaknesses.

Hurskainen (2009) describes a system for teaching Swahili, a language including noun classes and a complex agreement system. The system deals with morphological variation in a rule-governed way, as well as limited (concatenation based) syntax, including agreement. A learner may type some word-level input, such as a noun, and the system will analyze its morphological characteristics, indicating correctness, or an error message and a parse string. Learners may enter materials as they desire, depending on the constraints of the system, or may be taken on a 'guided tour', where they are prompted to produce increasingly more complex utterances (N, then N ADJ, and so on). Hurskainen's system has several advantages, including its encouragement of exploration by a learner, but several weaknesses as well. It appears to be limited strictly to orthographic input and output: other media like audio and images do not appear to be available. It is not clear how it could be modified without editing the grammatical representation, not a task accessible to typical instructors, and it is not clear whether it has been used in production.

Oahpa! (Antonsen, 2013; Antonsen et al., 2013) is a set of web-based language teaching materials for Northern Saami. It focusses on written activities including inflecting forms in isolation or in context, practicing simple lexical materials like numbers, and on basic question answering. Its lexicon includes basic semantic classification, phonotactic and morphophonological information, dialect information and translations to pivot languages. When the lexical database is generated, the morphological forms of words (including morphophonological variants) are also generated by the FST and saved in database tables, providing for detailed feedback on morphological errors. It is not clear, however, how that would deal with the variable placement of accented syllables in languages like Kanyen'kéha (see below). The contents of the lexicon are stored in XML, so that linguists familiar with that formalism can make changes, but it is not clear how new exercise types could be added. The results of user sessions are logged, permitting analysis of learner difficulties. It is claimed that the software is extensible to other languages.

In fact, the software behind Oahpa! has been adapted for the teaching of Plains Cree, under the title *nêhiyawêtân*. Bontogon (2016) has performed an analysis of its effectiveness using interviews with users and observation of use. While recognizing its value and potential, she flags up several issues, including interface issues (leftovers from the initial Finnish interface) and challenges to upkeep, since developers were not physically present, and it does not appear that teachers and students have the ability to change parameters or add features. To these comments, we would add the written-only character of input and output, and the still limited set of activities provided.

4   An alternative approach

In this section, we will present an alternative approach to language generation and CALL, designed to meet the desiderata mentioned in Section 2. The basic architecture is shown in Figure 1.

The three major components of the system include a natural language generator (**Vinci**) embedded in an editor (**ivi**), both written in C. The ivi editor may be used to edit both grammars and lexica. The stored language specifications are then used by Vinci to generate utterances on demand and to analyze student responses (Levison et al., 2001; Lessard and Levison, 2007). The ivi/Vinci system interacts with a user interface (**stdnt**), written in PHP, JavaScript, CSS and html5, responsible for presenting materials (written, audio, visual) to a learner within a web interface, and capturing and presenting to ivi/Vinci learner input for analysis. At the same time, a back end to the system (**instr**), written in PHP, provides grammatical and pedagogical direction to the process (what materials to produce, in what language, using what exercise format) as well as ensuring administrative tasks such as ensuring that learners are

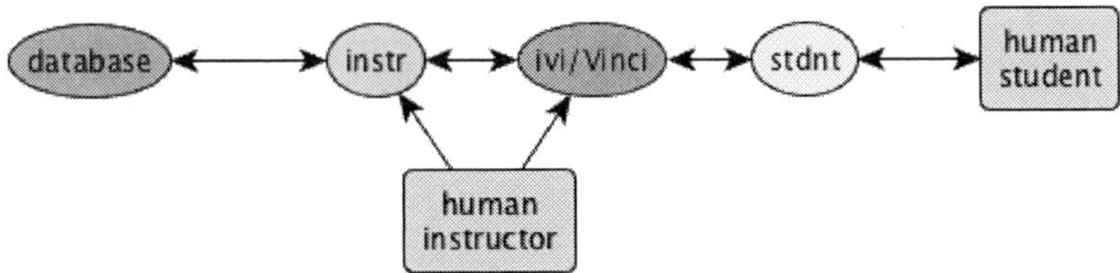

Figure 1: The architecture of the VinciLingua system

in particular classes, determining what exercises are available, and recording how individual learners have performed. The entire system is called **VinciLingua** (Lessard and Levison, 2018) and has been used successfully in production mode over the past four years by the office of Continuing and Distance Studies at Queen's University in Canada, in the context of two online French courses. Over the past year, we have been adapting the system for use in Kanyen'kéha, with a view to using it in a series of beginning University-level language and culture courses, the first of which will be taught in the fall of 2018.

The ivi/Vinci component makes use of a linguist-friendly set of metalanguages for specifying the elements of a language, including semantics, syntax, lexicon and morphology. More precisely, it is an attributed phrase structure grammar, enhanced with transformations, multipass morphological rules, and complex lexical entries, which may be preselected to drive syntactic choices. We provide here a more detailed view of how these elements work together.

4.1 Attributes and terminals

The basic building blocks of a grammar are a set of attributes and terminal symbols. The following is a simple attributes file for Kanyen'kéha:

```
PNG (p1s, p2s, p3sm, p3sf, p3si, p1d2, p1d3, p1p2, p1p3, p2d, p2p,
        p3dm, p3df, p3pm, p3pf)
Language (mohawk, english)
Meaning (action, negemotion, posemotion, poseval, negeval, state)
Medium (audio, image, text)
PrefType (ptense, pperson)
SuffType (stense)
Tense (present, past, future, conditional)
Stem (a_stem, c_stem, en_stem, i_stem, on_stem)
```

Attributes are composed of classes and values. Here, the class **PNG** represents the various persons available for pronominals in Kanyen'kéha, as in 'p1s' (first person singular), 'p2d' (second person dual), and so on. The class **Language** allows the generation of one root tree (see below) whose language is Kanyen'kéha, and another whose language is English. The **Meaning** class represents here a very basic ontology for verbs, including actions, negative emotions (for example, sadness), positive emotions, positive evaluations (think pretty, strong), and so on. Some attributes are used to control elements of morphology. Thus, **PrefType** allows the differentiation of pre-prenominal prefixes (like *en-*) for the future tense, and person pronominals (like *wak-*, 'to me'). The class **Tense** has the obvious meaning, while **Stem** allows the system to select particular classes of verbs based on their stem-type. Attributes may be partially ordered, so that, for example, both humans and animals are mobile, and compounded, as in 'action.past', to allow for dynamically richer sets. Finally, attributes may be used to control the medium of output, permitting the generation of parallel audio and textual elements, images and text, and so on.

The specification of terminals is very simple and consists in defining their labels, as in **V, PREF** and so on. Two special terminals, **BEGIN** and **END**, are used to mark the beginning and end of sequences; this is used in the dynamic calculation of accented syllables.

4.2 Lexical entries

The combination of attributes and terminals allows lexical entries to be defined. The following example shows an abbreviated form of a simple verbal entry as it would appear in the ivi editor:

```
1/HWord:   "na'khwen'on"{angry}
2/POS:     V
3/Attr:    c_stem, negemotion, PNG, Tense, Language, Medium
4/Freq :
5/LRule:   $v_conj
6/MRule:   $accentb
13/Prop:   cstem, p_hne, f_hake, s3, a12
17/Engl1:  $e_conj
18/Engl2:  "angry"
24/Rphn1:  "na'"
25/Rphn2:  "khwen"
26/Rphn3:  "'on"
27/TBD:
```

Each lexical entry represents an editable record in the lexicon, divided into fields. By definition, the first field contains the headword, followed by an English equivalent as a comment. This is followed by the part of speech (here **V**), and a set of attributes. We see that the verb is a c_stem verb which specifies a negative emotion, and that it can take all members of the class of Person, Tense and Gender, all tenses, all languages, and all media. (The use of the class in the lexicon rather than a value is the means of showing that all values are possible.)

Lexical entries may have **properties**, specific values which specify idiosyncratic elements which may be selected and used to determine choices during generation. So we see that this verb is a cstem verb, that its past tense suffix is -*hne* as opposed to other possibilities like -*hkwe* or -*hahkwe*. Information is also presented for English equivalents, including morphology rules and strings. The property **s3** indicates that this is a three syllable verb root, while the property **a12** shows that accent can occur on either the last or previous syllable (counting from end of word).

Fields 24, 25 and 26 are important. They contain, beginning in field 26 and counting backwards, the syllables which make up the verb. Division of each lexical entry into syllables is provided by an AWK script at the time of lexical entry, with subsequent human correction of the division.

4.3 Morphology rules

The Vinci system makes use of multiple pass morphology, where the output of one rule may be processed by a second rule[2]. In the case of the lexical entry above, two rules are called: **$v_conj** and **$accentb**. The first adds the basic form of the verb, and the second determines its form in context. This feature allows a morphology rule to select the appropriately accented syllable and to transform it by adding pitch and length markers, thus capturing an important feature of Kanyen'kéha: the accented syllable is determined by the number of following syllables, which depends in turn on the structure of the particular verbal complex. So in the past tense, where it is followed by -*hne*, *na'khwen'on* becomes *na'khwen'**ón**hne*, whereas in the present, it takes the form *na'**khwén**'on*.

We will illustrate the structure of a morphology rule with a simple partial example, designed to select the appropriate form of the duals meaning 'you and I' or 'someone and I'.

```
rule yonkeni
        english: #17;
        audio: #20;
        image: #21;
        1=<13=cstem> : "yonkeni";
        1=<13=astem> : "yonky";
        ...
%
```

The rule begins by checking for the attribute 'english'. If it finds it, the contents of field 17 in the lexical entry are output (here, the rule **$e_conj** which generates the equivalent English form or sequence). This

---

[2]This is similar in some respects to the TWOLC model found in FST.

allows for translation. If the attribute 'audio' is found, then the appropriate sound file will be called, and if the attribute 'image' is found, the appropriate image file is called for presentation on the screen. Otherwise, output will be in Kanyen'kéha. In that case, a check is done of the properties of the following item, here the verb. (In this system, 1=next, -1=previous, -2=second previous, and so on.) If the verb is of type `cstem`, then the pronominal takes the form *yonkeni*. If the verb is of type `astem` then the pronominal takes the form *yonky*, and so on.

4.4 Syntax rules

Syntactic rules in the system take the form of context-free phrase structure rules augmented by attributes, transformations, and lexical preselections. The object of this architecture is to provide maximum delicacy of generation, while retaining readability for non-programmer linguists writing grammars, since a small change at the top of the set of rules (in the preselection) can lead to significantly different output. We provide a simple example here:

```
PRESELECT =  a : V[past, p1s]/13=cstem/$0
%
ROOT =  SELECT Pe: PNG _in_ a, Te: Tense _in_ a;
   BEGIN
     PREF[ptense, Te]  PREF[pperson, Pe, Te]
     V[c_stem, Pe, Te]/_pre_ a  SUFF[stense, Te]
   END
%
QUESTION = ROOT %
ANSWER = MAKE_ENG:ROOT   %
MAKE_ENG = TRANSFORMATION
* PREF PREF V SUFF * : 1 2[english] 3[english] 4[english] 5[english] 6;
%
```

This small syntax may be divided into four parts: a **preselection**, **definition** of the ROOT tree, **transforms** of the ROOT to define a question and an answer, and **definitions** of the transformations themselves. We will take each in turn.

The preselection finds in the lexicon all forms which match its pattern, then randomly chooses one of the forms. Here, it is looking for a past tense first person singular verb, with the property 'cstem'. The frequency operator $0 at the end specifies that once each form has been found its frequency becomes zero, thus guaranteeing that it will not be used again. This is important in questions like multiple-choice, where all options should be different. It is also possible to alter frequency in other ways, by halving it, doubling it, and so on.

Once a verb has been chosen by a preselection, its values become available to the syntax. This allows the ROOT rule to **SELECT** for use the Person and Tense, give them labels (Pe and Te respectively) and attach these to nodes on the tree. Another operator _pre_ ensures that the verb itself in the root tree will be the one previously preselected.

The root tree itself is composed of the sequence BEGIN, PREF, PREF, V, SUFF, END, although it might in more complicated cases include branches and choices, as in any typical phrase structure grammar[3].

Note also that the terminal symbols BEGIN and END serve as markers for the attribution of accent, by providing an 'anchor' for the elements of the tree. The first PREF carries a tense marker, like *en-* to signal the certain future, the second carries the personal pronominal, like *wak-* to show the first person singular, which means, in the case of most stative verbs, something like 'to me'. The verb is obvious, while the SUFF carries a further tense marker, like *-hne*.

Specification of the ROOT is followed by creation of parallel trees for the question and expected answer. Here, the QUESTION tree is simply a copy of the root tree, while the ANSWER tree is obtained

---

[3]It is also important to note that it might have been possible to handle all elements of the verbal complex strictly within morphology rules, leaving syntax to handle combinations of words. We have not adopted this approach since it leads to extremely complex morphological rules, and since it complicates the option of creating parallel trees (see below). So in our system, syntax captures both the combination of separate lexical elements in an utterance, but also the structure of combined elements within the verbal complex.

by applying a transformation to the root. An indefinite number of parallel trees may be produced in order to model variant answers or to model expected errors.

Transformations (for example, here, `MAKE_ENG`) take the form of patterns and actions. Here, any sequence of `PREF PREF V SUFF`, with or without prior or following elements (indicated by the asterisks), will have the attribute 'english' attached to them, thus ensuring that the morphology rule will select the English form in the item's lexical entry.

In other words, this syntax carries the information: find a verb of such a type, make a tree by adding prefixes and suffixes, make copies of the tree, where the first copy is the question, and the second the expected answer, where the expected answer is the English equivalent of the verb.

The result of this is a series (in principle, indefinite in length) of generated questions and expected answers, as the following examples illustrate:

- Question : wakye'ónhne
  Answer : I was awake

- Question : wakerhá:rehkwe
  Answer : I was waiting

- Question : wake'nikonhren'tónhne
  Answer : I was depressed

Note that the question need not take the form of an actual question, but may be some textual, visual or audio element or set of elements presented to the learner for his or her reaction. Similarly, the answer may take the form of a written text, but images or to a limited extent sounds are also possible. Thus, one of the exercises available to learners shows pictures of animals and asks the learner to find the appropriate name. In an extension of this which we are beginning to explore, the system generates an utterance in Kanyen'kéha, for example *wake'nikonhren'tónhne* (='to me' + 'depressed' + 'past'), which forms the expected answer, and a series of stick images, which represent the meaning to be expressed: for example, a stick figure pointing at self + a sad face + an arrow pointing backwards, which form the question.

4.5 Evaluation of output

As noted earlier, the grammar and lexica for Kanyen'kéha are currently under development, for use in four courses to be taught over the next two years. It is estimated that on the order of 250 base (i.e. inflectable) forms will be used in each course, including nouns, verbal bases, prefixes and suffixes, for a total of approximately 1000 base forms. This is then not a large lexicon. However, with the inclusion of the appropriate syntactic and morphological rules, the number of potential forms rises significantly. In addition, as Snoek et al. (2014) have noted, once the basic rules have been created, addition of lexical materials becomes less complex.

For any generative system, evaluation of its (in principle indefinitely large) output must be found. In the case of VinciLingua, this is done in two ways. First, ivi/Vinci may be run in batch mode to output all forms of a structure into a spreadsheet, which may be reviewed by a human language expert. This is what is now done, and given the size of the current lexicon, it is still feasible. Second, on the language learning webpage itself, instructors may cause the system to generate sets of questions and answers and select only a subset to be shown to learners. This has been used regularly to produce quizzes in work on French.

5 Analysis of learner responses

In a software review, Dyck (2002) expresses frustration with a piece of language teaching software's requirement that a learner response match perfectly the expected pattern or be rejected. Beyond multiple choice, we would like more advanced learners to be able to type answers and have them diagnosed by the system.

One of the significant advantages of a generative approach is that it can make this possible by producing not only expected answers, but also by generating potential errors by rule, or, strictly speaking, by

malrule (Sleeman, 1982). Malrules may be thought of as rules which specify an expected error, or from another perspective, as representations in the mind of a student which produce erroneous output. The ivi/Vinci system caters for errors or variation in lexical choice, syntax, morphology, and orthography.

In the case of morphology, the system tests all variants of a morphological rule to determine whether a learner has mistakenly used the wrong variant. So in the case of the morphology rule for *yonkeni-*, all variant forms generated by the rule (*yonkeni-, yonky- yonken-*) are silently generated. If the learner's response does not match the expected correct form, it is compared to all silently generated forms. If one matches, it is presumed to be based on a malrule, and the appropriate error message can be generated, pointing out what the student has missed.

In the case of orthography, morphology rules may capture dialectal variation, which Harrigan et al. (2017) have flagged as a significant challenge to an FST, in several ways. Thus, within Kanyen'kéha, some dialects use the letter *y* while others use the letter *i*. This may be captured by means of a morphological rule **$y**, with attributes for each dialect, to generate either the string *y* or the string *i* and to signal changes from one to the other. Alternatively, since a Vinci lexicon includes **lexical pointers** to related forms such as spelling variants, synonyms, antonyms, or other related items, the dialectal variation found in the particle for 'something that must happen' which takes the form *tká:konte* in Tyendinaga, *ó:nen'k tsi* in Kahnawà:ke, or *entá:onk* in Kanehsatà:ke, may be captured by an addition to the various lexical entries, as in:

```
"tká:konte"|N|action, ....|dial1:"ó:nen'k tsi"; dial2:  "entá:onk"...
```

and so on, so that if a learner enters a dialectal variant of the expected word, the system can react appropriately, either accepting the variant without comment, or flagging up its difference.

In the case of syntax, transforms of the root tree (see above) may represent not only correct but also expected erroneous structures. So, for example, missing out a pre-pronominal tense marker may be captured by a transformation like:

```
NOTENSEPREF  = TRANSFORMATION
* PREF[ptense] * : 1 3 ;
%
```

Matches to erroneous transformations can be used as the starting point for error messages to the student. Similar rules may be used to capture mis-orderings of morphemes, or addition of spurious morphemes.

6 Multimedia and exploration

There exists some some limited evidence regarding the important role of accented syllables[4] in the acquisition of Kanyen'kéha. Thus Mithun (1989) studied five young speakers ranging in age from 1 to 5 and compared their use of complex polysynthetic forms. She found that the youngest speaker tended to retain and produce the accented syllable, responding to phonological salience; somewhat older speakers moved progressively leftward in complex forms, adding additional syllables; and the oldest speaker had reached the pronominal form and appears to be using rudimentary morphological rules.

But what of L2 learners? On the basis of classroom intuitions, we hypothesize that syllables will form an important early step and should be made as salient as possible. To capture syllables and longer oral utterances, we make use of web-based recording, followed by automatic post-processing using the **sox** software. The resulting sound files may be associated with their orthography in tables, so that a learner can click on sets to learn patterns, as Figure 2, taken from a webpage, illustrates.

At the same time, the soundfiles for syllables may also be reused by an ivi/Vinci grammar, so that output of a set of rules is composed of one or more soundfiles played on a webpage. This permits a pedagogical trajectory, with tables being followed by simple exercises based on listening and differentiating individual syllables, as in Figure 3, more complex exercises where, given a full pronominal/verbal complex, a learner must identify meaning, as in Figure 4, or even more complex activities involving writing the equivalent of an oral utterance (in French, the 'dictée').

---

[4]Of course, accented syllables are only a small part of acquisition in polysynthetic languages. For example, Allen et al. (in press) have developed test procedures for Inuktitut which analyze multiple dimensions.

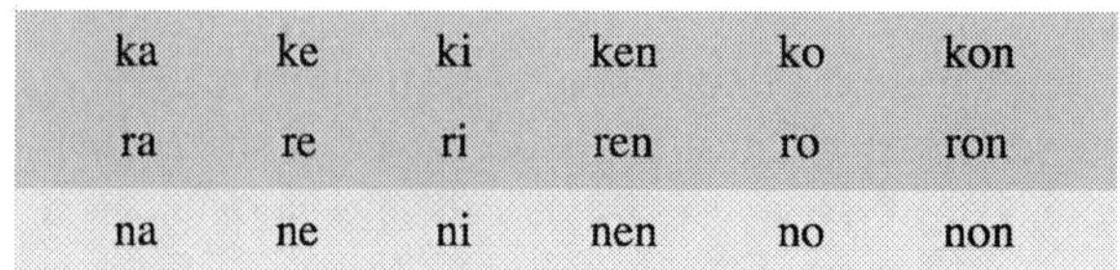

Figure 2: A (partial) syllable table for exploration

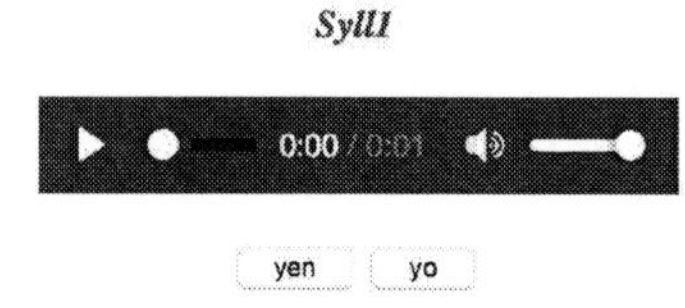

Figure 3: An exercise to practice syllable differentiation

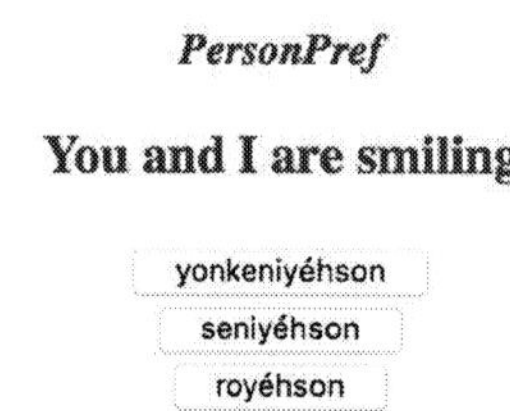

Figure 4: An exercise to identify verbal forms

7   Conclusions and Future Work

The crucial conclusions of the work described here are these:

- a generative approach, combined with the use of varied media, including sounds and images, represents a significant economy of effort in the production of the forms of Kanyen'kéha, and potentially for other polysynthetic languages;

- because the same grammar may underlie different activities, it is possible to define a trajectory for learners, starting with exploration of oral and written materials, to differentiation, then analysis and (at least in writing) production, while associating learner divergences from the target with tendencies to be addressed either in teaching materials or in class;

- at the same time, a generative approach, while valuable, must be included in a broader sequence of activities including cultural knowledge, texts, and activities in the language, both in and out of the classroom. This includes folktales and legends (Shakokwenionkwas, 2008; Williams, 1976), which we have not touched on here.

Acknowledgements

The work described here is a result of a partnership between Tsi Tyónnheht Onkwawén:na Language and Cultural Centre on the Tyendinaga Mohawk Territory, and Queen's University at Kingston, including the office of Continuing and Distance Studies, the School of Computing, and the Department of Languages, Literatures and Cultures, with funding provided by the Province of Ontario. We would also like to thank the anonymous reviewers for their valuable comments.

References

Shanley E. M. Allen, Catherine B. Dench, and Kerry Isakson. in press. InuLARSP: An Adaptation of the Language Assessment Remediation and Screening Procedure for Inuktitut. In M.J. Ball, D. Crystal, and P. Fletcher, editors, *Assessing grammar: Even more languages of LARSP*. Multilingual Matters, Clevedon, UK.

Lene Antonsen, Ryan Johnson, Trond Trosterud, and Heli Uibo. 2013. Generating modular grammar exercises with finite-state transducers. In *Proceedings of the second workshop on NLP for computer-assisted language learning at NODALIDA 2013*, number 17 in NEALT Proceedings Series, pages 27–38. Linköping Electronic Conference Proceedings 86.

Lene Antonsen. 2013. Constraints in free-input question-answering drills. In *Proceedings of the second workshop on NLP for computer-assisted language learning at NODALIDA 2013*, number 17 in NEALT Proceedings Series, pages 11–26, Linköping Electronic Conference Proceedings 86.

Marion Bittinger. 2006. Software helps revitalize use of Mohawk language. *Multilingual Magazine*, pages 59–61.

Megan Bontogon. 2016. Evaluating nêhiyawêtân: A computer assisted language learning (CALL) application for Plains Cree. Master's thesis, University of Alberta.

Nancy Bonvillain and Beatrice Francis. 1972. *A Mohawk and English Dictionary*. New York State Education Department, Albany.

Nancy Bonvillain. 1973. *A grammar of Akwesasne Mohawk*. Number 8 in Ethnology Division, Mercury Series. National Museum of Man, Ottawa.

Nora Deering and Helga Harries-Delisle. 2007. *Mohawk: a teaching grammar*. Kanien'kehá:ka Onkwawén:na Raotitióhwka Language and Cultural Center, Kahnawàke, 2nd edition.

Carrie Dyck. 2002. Review of Tsi Karhakta: At The Edge of the Woods. *Language Learning & Technology*, 6(2):27–33.

Joshua A. Fishman. 1991. *Reversing language shift: theoretical and empirical foundations of assistance to threatened languages*. Multilingual Matters, Clevedon.

Claire Gardent and German Kruszewski. 2012. Generation for Grammar Engineering. In *INLG 2012, The seventh International Natural Language Generation Conference*, pages 31–40.

Jeremy Green. 2017. Pathways to creating Onkwehonwehnéha speakers at Six Nations of The Grand River Territory. Technical report, Six Nations Polytechnic.

Atticus G. Harrigan, Katherine Schmirler, Antti Arppe, Lene Antonsen, Trond Trosterud, and Arok Wolvengrey. 2017. Learning from the computational modelling of Plains Cree verbs. *Morphology*, 27:565–598.

Michael Hoover. 1992. The revival of the Mohawk language in Kahnawake. *Canadian Journal of Native Studies*, 12(2):269–287.

Arvi Hurskainen. 2009. Intelligent Computer-Assisted Language Learning: Implementation to Swahili. Technical report, Institute for Asian and African Studies; University of Helsinki, http://www.njas.helsinki.fi/salama.

Maddalen Lopez de Lacalle Itziar Aldabe, Montse Mar-Itxalar, Edurne Martínez, and Larraitz Uria. 2006. Arikiturri: an automatic question generator based on corpora and NLP techniques. In *Proceedings of the 8th international conference on Intelligent Tutoring Systems, ITS'06*, pages 584–594, Berlin, Heidelberg. Springer-Verlag.

David Kanatawakhon-Maracle, 2002. *Tsi Karhakta: At The Edge of the Woods (Mohawk courseware)*.

David Kanatawakhon. 2013a. *To I'i Tewaweyentehta'n ne Kanyen'keha. Let's learn Mohawk: an introductory grammar text for learning the Mohawk language*. Centre for Research and Teaching of Canadian Native Languages, University of Western Ontario, London, ON.

David Kanatawakhon. 2013b. *To I'i Tewaweyentehta'n ne Kanyen'keha. Let's learn Mohawk: a text of grammar supplements concerning nominals*. Centre for Research and Teaching of Canadian Native Languages, University of Western Ontario, London, ON.

Sarah Kell. 2014. Polysynthetic Language Structures and their Role in Pedagogy and Curriculum for BC Indigenous Languages: Final Report. Technical report, British Columbia Ministry of Education.

Greg Lessard and Michael Levison. 2007. Lexical creativity in L2 French and Natural Language Generation. In Dalilah Ayoun, editor, *French Applied Linguistics*, pages 299–333. John Benjamins.

Greg Lessard and Michael Levison. 2018. Vincilingua website. `https://vincilingua.ca`.

Michael Levison, Greg Lessard, Anna Marie Danielson, and Delphine Merven. 2001. From Symptoms to Diagnosis. In Keith Cameron, editor, *CALL - The Challenge of Change*, pages 53–59.

M. Paul Lewis and Gary F. Simons. 2010. Assessing Endangerment: Expanding Fishman's Grids. *Revue Roumaine de Linguistique*, LV(2):103–120.

David Kanatawakhon Maracle. 2001. *Mohawk Language Thematic Dictionary*. Kanyen'keha Books, London, ON.

Mary McDonald. 1977. *Iontenwennaweienstahkhwa': Mohawk Spelling Dictionary*, volume Bulletin 429. New York State Museum, Albany.

Gunther Michelson. 1973. *A thousand words of Mohawk*. Number 5 in Ethnology Division, Mercury Series. National Museum of Man, Ottawa.

Marianne Mithun. 1984. The Proto-Iroquoians: Cultural reconstruction from lexical materials. In Jack Campisi, Michael K. Foster, and Marianne Mithun, editors, *Extending the Rafters*, pages 259–282. SUNY Press, Albany.

Marianne Mithun. 1989. The acquisition of polysynthesis. *Journal of Child Language*, 16:285–312.

Marianne Mithun. 2006. The Iroquoian languages. In *Encyclopedia of Language and Linguistics*, volume 6, pages 31–34. Elsevier, Oxford, 2nd edition.

Barry M. Montour. 2012. The Kanien'kéha Proficiency Assessment. In *First Nations Lifelong Learning Assessment Report*, pages 22–27.

Laura Perez-Beltrachini, Claire Gardent, and German Kruszewski. 2012. Generating Grammar Exercises. In *The 7th Workshop on the Innovative Use of NLP for Building Educational Applications*, pages 147–156. Association for Computational Linguistics.

Tom Porter Shakokwenionkwas. 2008. *And Grandma Said... Iroquois Teachings*. Private publication, Kanatsiohareke Mohawk Community, Fonda, New York.

Derek Sleeman. 1982. An attempt to understand students' understanding of basic algebra. *Cognitive Science*, 8(4):387–412.

Conor Snoek, Dorothy Thunder, Kaidi Lõo, Antti Arppe, Jordan Lachler, Sjur Moshagen, and Trond Trosterud. 2014. Modeling the Noun Morphology of Plains Cree. In *Proceedings of the 2014 workshop on the use of computational methods in the study of endangered languages*, pages 34–42. Association for Computational Linguistics.

Kahtehrón:ni Iris Stacey. 2016. Ientsitewate'nikonhraié:ra'te tsi nonkwá:ti ne á:se tahatikonhsontóntie: We will turn our minds there once again, to the faces yet to come. Master's thesis, University of Victoria.

Marianne Williams, editor. 1976. *Kanien'kéha' Okara'shón:'a (Mohawk Stories)*, volume 427, Albany. New York State Museum.

Kawennón:nis: the Wordmaker for Kanyen'kéha

Anna Kazantseva
National Research Council Canada
anna.kazantseva@nrc-cnrc.gc.ca

Owennatekha Brian Maracle
Onkwawenna Kentyohkwa
owennatekha@gmail.com

Ronkwe'tiyóhstha Josiah Maracle
Onkwawenna Kentyohkwa
diotsta@gmail.com

Aidan Pine
National Research Council Canada
aidan.pine@nrc-cnrc.gc.ca

Abstract

In this paper we describe preliminary work on *Kawennón:nis*, a verb conjugator for Kanyen'kéha (Ohsweken dialect). The project is the result of a collaboration between Onkwawenna Kentyohkwa Kanyen'kéha immersion school and the Canadian National Research Council's Indigenous Language Technology lab.

The purpose of Kawennón:nis is to build on the educational successes of the Onkwawenna Kentyohkwa school and develop a tool that assists students in learning how to conjugate verbs in Kanyen'kéha; a skill that is essential to mastering the language. Kawennón:nis is implemented with both web and mobile front-ends that communicate with an application programming interface that in turn communicates with a symbolic language model implemented as a finite state transducer. Eventually, it will serve as a foundation for several other applications for both Kanyen'kéha and other Iroquoian languages.

1 Introduction

Kanyen'kéha is an Iroquoian language, commonly known as "Mohawk", spoken in parts of Canada (Ontario and Quebec) and the United States (New York state). It has a vibrant community of learners, and educators but only about 3,500 L1 (first-language) speakers. Three main dialects are currently in use: Western (Ohsweken and Kenhteke), Eastern (Kahnawake, Kanehsatake and Wahta) and Central (Akwesasne). In our current work we focus exclusively on the Western dialect as spoken in Ohsweken.

The Truth and Reconciliation Committee of Canada led an inquiry into the atrocities committed during the residential school era in Canada from 1883 to the late 1990s. In 2015, they released a report (TRC, 2015) containing 94 calls to action, among them five action items that are related to Indigenous languages and culture. The report confirmed a macabre reality of residential schools that Indigenous people have known all along, that the residential school system was "created for the purpose of separating Aboriginal children from their families, in order to minimize and weaken family ties and cultural linkages" (TRC, 2015).

Since the release of the TRC report, a number of governmental and non-governmental programs and initiatives aimed at supporting Indigenous languages in Canada have been started. This project is a part of the National Research Council's (further *NRC*) related initiative to research and develop Indigenous language technology[1].

Despite the disproportionate duress that speakers of Indigenous languages have endured at the hands of Canadian colonial policies, the resilience and tenacity of Indigenous language communities can be seen in the myriad ways that they have resisted and continued to teach, learn and speak their languages (Pine and Turin, 2017, for further discussion). One such initiative is that of Onkwawenna Kentyohkwa, described in depth in Section 4. Given the widely celebrated accomplishments of Onkwawenna Kentyohkwa for almost two decades, it is apparent that it will be successful with or without the assistance of

[1]For more information about the project see www.nrc-cnrc.gc.ca/eng/solutions/collaborative/indigenous_languages/index.html

Proceedings of Workshop on Polysynthetic Languages, pages 53–64
Santa Fe, New Mexico, USA, August 20-26, 2018.

technology. It is therefore the goal of Kawennón:nis to develop a fundamentally assistive reference tool that doesn't *replace* learners' experience of acquiring Kanyen'kéha verbal morphology at Onkwawenna Kentyohkwa, but that *augments* and *complements* it.

Another factor contributing to the technological inequity faced by second-language learners of Kanyen'kéha compared with learners of more resourced languages is the result of the text-based bias of contemporary language technologies. Similar to most other Indigenous languages of North America, Kanyen'kéha acquired a standardized orthography recently (1993), relative to the multi-millennial history of the language's oral tradition. Dialectal differences, variations in spelling and the general paucity of written content in the language make statistical language learning difficult. The situation is particularly dire for the Western dialect: very little text is available in the Ohsweken dialect of Kanyen'kéha apart from Onkwawenna Kentyohkwa's curricular materials.

Most Indigenous languages in Eastern, Central and Northern Canada show high levels of polysynthesis, that is, their words are composed of relatively many morphemes. All Iroquoian languages fall into this category. Single words in Kanyen'kéha are routinely translated as entire sentences in English. For example:

(1) *enhake'serehtsherakwatákwahse-'*
     en-hake-'serehtsher-kwatakw-ahse-'
     will-he.to.me-car-fix.it.up-for.me-punctual
     FUT-3SG.M/1SG-fix.it.up-BEN-PUNC

     'he will repair my car for me'

(2) *tetsyonkyathahahkwahnónhne*
     te-ts-yonky-at-hahahkw-hnón-hne
     both-again-it.to.you.and.I-each.other-walk-purposive-have.gone
     DUAL-REP-3SG.N/1.DU.INCL-SREFL-walk-PURP-PPFV

     'the two of us went for a walk'

The generative power and compositional morphology of the language is such that neologisms are easily created, with no borrowing necessary. For example, the word for *pizza* is *teyotena'tarahwe'nón:ni* which literally means *round bread*. However, this property also makes the language difficult to teach, as learners cannot be expected to memorize paradigms arbitrarily. Rather, they must learn the patterns to *generate* the paradigms. This is the essential insight on which the morpheme-based teaching approach adopted by the Onkwawenna Kentyohkwa is based (see Section 4). The fact that there are 72 distinct bound pronominal morphemes in Kanyen'kéha means that even learning how to properly conjugate a modest number of verbs requires a significant amount of work. Kawennón:nis is a tool designed to help students with this task. It allows a user to enter a number of variables which the software then processes and outputs the corresponding grammatical form.

To the best of our knowledge, textual data in the Ohsweken dialect of Kanyen'kéha available publicly is quite scarce. Accordingly, we were not able to identify a sufficiently large corpus to use with statistical methods. The Ohsweken dialect also has less linguistic documentation than the Eastern and Central dialects which have been studied more extensively (Postal, 1963; Bonvillain, 1973; Beatly, 1974; Mithun, 2004). However, Onkwawenna Kentyohkwa has created a textbook (Maracle, 2017) that describes and explains salient morphological properties of Kanyen'kéha as spoken in Ohsweken. The textbook, along with linguistic sources about other dialects of Kanyen'kéha and the closely related language Oneida are the primary sources of information for creating the symbolic language model of Ohsweken Kanyen'kéha.

We see the main contributions of this work as follows. Successful collaborations between Indigenous communities and technology partners are rare. Perhaps the single most important contribution of this work is that it gives an example of a productive, harmonious collaboration between an immersion school within an Indigenous community (Onkwawenna Kentyohkwa) and a research group from outside the community (NRC). Details of this collaboration are discussed in Section 4.

Secondly, Kanyen'kéha has very little software support. Apart from LanguageGeek[2] and FirstVoices[3] keyboards there is no software that enables use of the language on desktops or on mobile devices. It is therefore a second important contribution of this work that we are creating the first computational language model of Kanyen'kéha.

The third contribution is in the applications, though at present these are prototypes and proofs of concept. Creating a symbolic language model is time consuming and error-prone. The finite state transducer behind Kawennón:nis is currently used for the verb conjugator and a limited spell-checker but in future, we hope to add other applications, thereby maximally leveraging the time and effort involved in making Kawennón:nis.

This paper is structured as follows. In Section 2 we place our project in the context of related research. In Section 3 we provide a high-level sketch of the relevant Kanyen'kéha verbal paradigms. Section 4 describes the immersion school Onkwawenna Kentyohkwa, the unique immersion teaching method it uses and the collaboration with NRC. Section 5 provides an overview of the software architecture of Kawennón:nis. In Section 6 we describe the symbolic language model that we have created. Section 7 talks about two prototype applications implemented to date and includes a brief discussion of evaluation. Finally, we discussing future Work in Section 8 and provide conclusions in Section 9.

2   Related Work

In this section we will list some of the relevant computational systems. Our work also heavily depends on linguistic sources (Lounsbury, 1953; Postal, 1963; Bonvillain, 1973; Beatly, 1974; Mithun, 1996; Mithun, 2004)). Furthermore, many language activists, teachers, students have made important contributions which, for the most part, are not available for citing.

While in general it is true that Indigenous languages lack adequate linguistic software support, our work relies on previous computational and linguistic research.

Moshagen et al. (2013) describe Giella - a framework for FST-based modeling of languages with the aim of easily creating end-user applications. The Giella infrastructure has been successfully used to create FSTs and corresponding tools for a number of languages: Cree (Snoek et al., 2014; Harrigan et al., 2017), Northern Haida (Lachler et al., 2018), Odawa (Bowers et al., 2017) are but a few of the many examples.

In a different line of work Littell et al. (2017) have created a tool called *Mother Tongues Dictionaries* (formerly *Waldayu*) that helps communities create web and mobile dictionaries from potentially heterogeneous community resources. The mobile version is used as the mobile front end for the extensive FirstVoices resources (Brand et al., 2015) .

For Indigenous languages where it is realistic to collect sufficient data, statistical modeling has been used successfully. Martin et al. (2003; Désilets et al. (2008) use parallel English-Inuktitut corpora to create translation memories and Micher (2017) uses a monolingual corpus of Inuktitut to improve the performance of a morphological analyzer.

For a recent survey of language technologies for Indigenous languages in Canada see (Littell et al., forthcoming). A more extensive inventory of open-source resources, in both Indigenous and other languages, is available at `github.com/RichardLitt/endangered-languages`.

Our work is most similar to that of Snoek et al. (2014; Harrigan et al. (2017; Lachler et al. (2018; Bowers et al. (2017). Kawennón:nis is somewhat similar to morphologically-aware dictionaries, but its design and content is far more customized.

---

[2] `http://www.languagegeek.com/rotinonhsonni/keyboards/iro_keyboards.html`
[3] http://www.firstvoices.com/en/apps

Figure 1: Examples of bound pronouns in Kanyen'kéha

Bound pronoun in Kanyen'kéha	English translation	Example (Kanyen'kéha)	Example (English)
ke-	me to it	**ke**khón:nis	I cook
ra-	he to it	**ra**khón:nis	he cooks
yonkeni-	it to me and you (or smb.)	**yonkeni**nòn:we's	it likes us (both)
yako-	it to her	**yako**nòn:we's	it likes her
take-	you to me	**take**nòn:we's	you like me
she-	you to her	**she**nòn:we's	you like her

3   Kanyen'kéha, the language of the Kanyen'kehá:ka

Kanyen'kéha[4] is part of the Iroquoian language family[5]. Two main subgroups of the Iroquoian language family are distinguished: the Southern Iroquoian (now only containing Cherokee) and Northern Iroquoian (Cayuga, Onondaga, Seneca, Mohawk (Kanyen'kéha), Oneida, Wyandot, Nottoway and Tuscarora) (Mithun, 2004). Wyandot is currently often considered a sleeping language, but see (Lukaniec, 2010) for very promising reclamation and revitalization work.

Kanyen'kéha has 11 consonants[6] /h/, /k/, /n/, /r/, /s/, /t/, /w/, /y/, /ts/, /k^w/, and /ʔ/ (Mithun, 2004) and 6 vowels /a/, /e/, /i/, /o/, /ʌ̃/, and /õ/[7]. Vowels can be marked for stress (´) and falling tone (`); both stress and falling tone can be marked for length (:) (Mithun, 1996).

A pronominal prefix, a verb root and an aspectual ending are always present (for commands the aspectual ending is null). A verb can contain pre- and post-pronominal prefixes and pre-aspectual suffixes. Verb roots are also bound morphemes and do not, on their own, constitute well-formed words.

Kanyen'kéha has 15 stand-alone or *free pronouns*, and 72 *bound pronouns* which can only be used as a part of a verb. Bound pronouns in Kanyen'kéha are very complex (Mithun, 1996). In one morphological unit, a pronoun encodes information about both the agent and the patient of an action. For both the agent and the patient, it also captures gender (male, female, neuter), number (single, dual or plural) and whether the hearer is included in the set (inclusivity). If no agent or patient is available, the pronoun is the same as the single neuter pronoun.

Some example pronouns are shown in Figure 1. The bound pronouns are divided into three groups: active pronouns (3; roughly for situations where the actor is human, and the patient is not, or where there is no patient), passive pronouns (4; for situations where the patient is human and the agent is not) and "transitive" pronouns (5; for situations when both the actor and the patient are human). Below are some examples:

(3)   *Senòn:wes*
    se-nonhwe'n-s
    you.to.it-like-habitual
    2.SG.AGENT-like-HAB

    '**You** like it.'

(4)   *Sanòn:wes*
    sa-nonhwe'n-s
    it.to.you-like-habitual
    2.SG.PATIENT-like-HAB

    '**It** likes you.'

---

[4]ISO 639-2 code is *moh*.

[5]In this Section and further in this paper we are sometimes faced with the choice of whether to use standardized terminology from Linguistics, or to rely on the knowledge of the community. Almost exclusively, we use the terminology and categories as described in (Maracle, 2017). We made this decision because the textbook is the most detailed and accurate description of the Ohsweken dialect available to-date and because the theoretical understandings of the textbook form the basis of our language model.

[6]These are represented orthographically and taught as 8 consonants, h, k, n, r, s, t, w, y, plus glottal stop ' (Maracle, 2017).

[7]These are represented orthographically as a, e, i, o, en, on respectively.

(5) *Takenòn:wes*
     take-nonhwe'n-s
     you.to.me-like-habitual
     2.SG/1.SG-like-HAB

     '**You** like **me**.'

In reality, the situation is not quite this simple: in many cases, the choice of a pronoun is lexicalized and determined more by the history of a specific verb or by traditional usage than by tangible properties of the actor or the patient.

For instance the verb *rihwayent* meaning 'decide' as seen in example 6 below uses patientive pronouns (in this case *wake*, roughly meaning *it to me*.)

(6) *ya'tewakerihwayentà:ses*
     y-a'-te-wake-rihwayent-'se-s
     there-did-it.to.me-decide-for.me-habitual
     TRANS-FACT-1.SG.PATIENT-business.matters-decide-BEN-HAB

     'I decided.'

There are 11 possible pre-pronominal prefixes and a verb can take on one or more of them. Some possible prefixes are the definite (7), cislocative (8), translocative (9), and many others. For example:

(7) *Wa'katáweya'te'*
     wa'-k-ataweya't-e'
     did-I.to.it-enter.a.place-punctual
     FACT-1.SG.AGENT-enter.a.place-PUNC

     'I entered (a place).'

(9) *Ya'katáweya'te'*
     y-a'-k-ataweya't-e'
     there-did-I.to.it-enter.a.place-punctual
     TRANS-FACT-1.SG.AGENT-enter.a.place-PUNC

     'I went in (**there**).'

(8) *Takatáweya'te'*
     t-a-k-ataweya't-e'
     here-did.here-I.to.it-enter.a.place-punctual
     CIS-FACT-1.SG.AGENT-enter.a.place-PUNC

     'I came in (**here**).'

A verb may also take one of the three pre-aspectual case suffixes (Beatly, 1974). For example the distributive (11), reversive (12) or purposive (13):

(10) *Enkhnyó:ten'*
      en-k-hnyot-en'
      will-I-stand.up-punctual
      FUT-1SG.AGENT-stand.up-PUNC

      'I will stand it up.'

(12) *Enkhnyotá:ko'*
      en-k-hnyot-**ako**-'
      will-I-stand.up-**reversive**-punctual
      FUT-1SG.AGENT-stand.up-**REV**-PUNC

      'I will **lower** it.'

(11) *Enkhnyónnyon'*
      en-k-hnyot-**onnyon**-'
      will-I-stand.up-**distributive**-punctual
      FUT-1SG.AGENT-stand.up-**DIST**-PUNC

      'I will stand **many things** up.'

(13) *Enkhnyotà:na'*
      en-k-hnyot-**ahn**-a'
      will-I-stand.up-**purposive**-punctual
      FUT-1SG.AGENT-stand.up-**PURP**-PUNC

      'I will **go** stand it up.'

The stem of a verb can also be complex due to noun incorporation. In the current version of Kawennón:nis we only cover a limited set of paradigms: namely the mandatory parts of the verb (the pronominal prefix, the root and the aspectual ending). In the coming months, we will extend our model to all paradigms that do not require semantic restrictions.

4   Collaboration between NRC & Onkwawenna Kentyohkwa

Onkwawenna Kentyohkwa is an adult immersion program in southern Ontario that was founded in 1999. The program currently teaches a two-year program that enables students to achieve high levels of proficiency in Kanyen'kéha (the "Mohawk" language). Students attend six hours per day, five days a week, for two school years, totaling 2,000 hours of instruction, all in the language.

The program uses a unique morpheme-based teaching method that allows students with little or no previous language exposure to achieve one of the Advanced levels on oral proficiency assessments based on the American Council on Teaching of Foreign Languages model (Breiner-Sanders et al., 2000). A few graduates are now raising children as first-language speakers.

The program's success has generated interest across the continent and adult groups from other Iroquois communities (Oneida and Seneca) have translated the curriculum and materials into their languages to teach adults in their communities.

The idea behind creating Kawennón:nis, originated with a staff member of the Onkwawenna Kentyohkwa School. Thus, the Onkwawenna Kentyohkwa school defined the scope and the main parts of Kawennón:nis, motivated by a specific educational need that the staff of Onkwawenna Kentyohkwa identified as important.

In order to move ahead with the project in a collaborative fashion, NRC partnered with a staff member of the school who participated in ongoing correspondence and communication, including weekly online meetings to discuss the user interface of Kawennón:nis and to make decisions regarding morphology. Additionally, members of NRC have made several in-person visits to Ohsweken to demonstrate Kawennón:nis to students and staff of Onkwawenna Kentyohkwa and to participate in intensive, multi-day, collaborative efforts brainstorming project decisions and direction as well as designing the user interfaces. This level of mutual collaboration and continual involvement from both NRC and Onkwawenna Kentyohkwa will be essential if the project is to succeed.

5   Kawennón:nis: Overview

Kawennón:nis is built with the hope of supporting a wide variety of user applications, and of eventually extending it to use with other Iroquoian languages. It consists of three main parts: (1) a 'frontend' implemented with Angular and Ionic for the web, as well as Android and iOS platforms. (2) An API implemented in Python (Flask). (3) a 'backend' consisting of a finite state transducer implemented in Foma (Hulden, 2009). This architecture allows alternate frontends or future iterations of the current frontend tools to make use of the FST. It also gives a clear point of integration for FSTs of other Iroquoian languages. This section describes the software architecture for Kawennón:nis as illustrated in Figure 2.

Figure 2: Kawennón:nis system architecture from back to front.

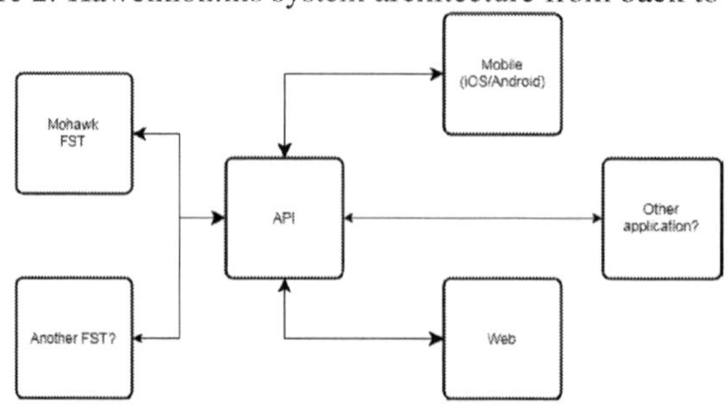

5.1 API

The Kawennón:nis API (Application Programming Interface) is used to define the methods through which frontend components or applications like websites or mobile apps may interact with the backend FST. The API is read-only, requires an API-key to be accessed and follows RESTful design principles, whereby the API is stateless, cacheable, decoupled from the FST and frontend applications as much as possible and exposes information about available verbs, pronouns, conjugated forms and other data as discrete resources and subresources.

5.2 Web & mobile applications

The user interface for both web and mobile frontends have the same core components. First, a 'conjugation' component which renders the API response on a number of different user-defined tiers. Second, a 'palette' component which allows the user to set the parameters for the request to the API. Below in Figure 3 the conjugation component can be seen on the left and the palette component on the right.

Additionally, the user has control over which parts in the conjugation to highlight. The Onkwawenna Kentyohkwa immersion school uses a colour scheme where agents are highlighted in red, patients in blue and transitive pronouns are highlighted in purple. For ensuring an easy transition between the course and Kawennón:nis, this colour scheme is preserved in Kawennón:nis and the user can optionally select whether to also colour-code the verb stem or various other types of affixes (aspectual suffixes, for example). The user is also able to select between a variety of tiers to display in the conjugation component. The first, main tier is the orthographic word without any segmentation. The next tiers that are available include a morpheme breakdown tier, and two type glossing tiers, one which simply glosses all morphemes by their category (ie 'pronoun', 'root' etc.) and another which gives the English gloss (ie. 'you', 'cook' etc.). Users are anonymously authenticated and their settings are saved across sessions on the same devices.

6 Symbolic Model of Verbal Morphology in Kanyen'kéha

The backbone of Kawennón:nis is a symbolic model of the Kanyen'kéha verbal morphology implemented as a *finite state transducer* (further *FST*).

A finite state transducer is a type of finite state automaton that maps between two sets of states: the input set and the output set. The sets of states are often referred to as the input and output alphabets. The transducer can be thought of as a "translating machine": it translates an input sequence into an output one. In our context, the FST first translates a sequence specifying 1) the verb stem and 2) a set of tags capturing the desired morphological properties, and then it outputs a verb correct form.

Formally, an FST is a seven-tuple $(Q, \Sigma, \Gamma, \delta, w, I, F)$ such that Q is the finite set of all possible states, Σ is the finite set of all possible input symbols – the input alphabet, Γ is the finite set of all possible output

Figure 3: The Kawennón:nis web application

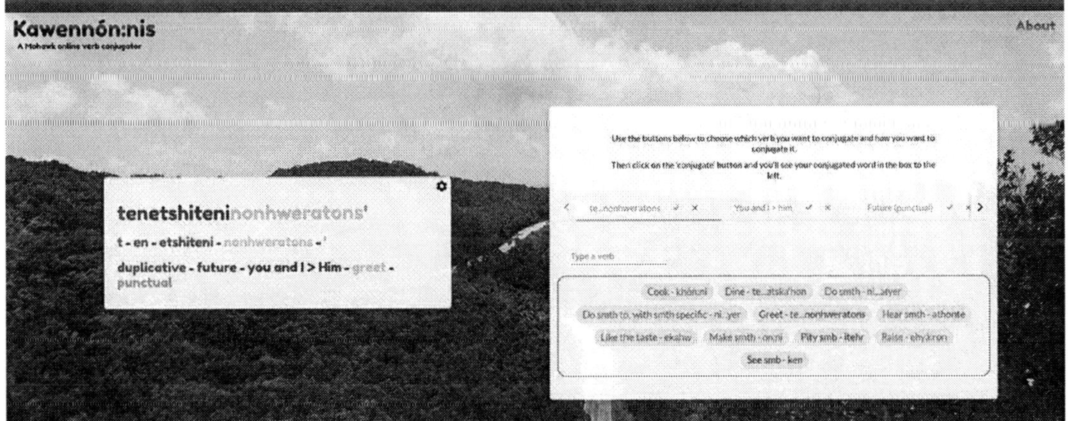

symbols – the output alphabet, $\delta : Q \times \Sigma \to Q$ is the transition function, $w : Q \times \Sigma \to \Gamma$ is the output function, $I \subset Q$ is the set of initial states and $F \subset Q$ is the set of accepting states (Mohri, 1997).

For example, a toy FST for a subset of conjugations of the verb *cook* is shown in Figure 4 below. Example 14 below is a demonstration of the valid input mappings to the corresponding output sequences.

(14)   *a.*   cook+3rd $\to$ cooks

       b.   cook+Past $\to$ cooked

       c.   kick+Participle $\to$ kicking

In general even if the morphological paradigms that are encoded are complex, adding new verbs is simple and straightforward.

Following the convention (Beesley and Karttunen, 2003; Koskenniemi, 1986), we separate lexical and morphological rules from phonological alternations in our implementation. The latter are applied as a second layer. The rules are implemented as a continuation lexicon in *lexc* formalism and the phonological alternations as rewrite rules, both of which are implemented in Foma (Hulden, 2009). See Beesley and Karttunen (2003) for a discussion on structuring linguistic FSTs.

Creating a linguistic FST involves manually hand-coding all morphological rules - a very time-consuming and potentially error-prone process. A more contemporary alternative would be to learn morphology from a corpus. However, we are unaware of any sufficiently large, homogeneous corpus of Kanyen'kéha; nor are we aware of any corpus at all for the Ohsweken dialect. On the other hand, some linguistic documentation for Kanyen'kéha is available (Beatly, 1974; Bonvillain, 1973; Postal, 1963; Mithun, 1996; Mithun, 2004). The root-word method textbook (Maracle, 2017), the linguistic sources listed above and continuous input from a proficient speaker of Kanyen'kéha[8] have been our main sources of information.

The FST is structured so that adding new verbs is fast and painless: it amounts to entering a lexical entry into a spreadsheet and specifying several properties. The input, collation and quality control of this task is done by both NRC researchers and teachers at Onkwawenna Kentyohkwa.

Long-distance dependencies complicate the otherwise relatively straightforward structure of morphological rules. While there are no true long-distance dependencies, the selectional preferences of verbs are treated *like* long-distance dependencies by the *lexc* formalism. Some examples are restrictions on what type of bound pronoun can be used with a given verb, the conjugation class of a verb or the presence of a mandatory prefix. We model such dependencies using flag diacritics.

Phonological alternations are yet another challenge. For example, each of the 72 possible bound pronouns changes depending on which sound follows it.[9] Five major categories can be distinguished (verb stems that start with a consonant, an "a", "e", "i", or an "o"). However, there are numerous exceptions to this which makes encoding phonological rules non-trivial.

---

[8]The 3rd author of this paper.

[9]In the current version of Kawennón:nis this placeholder can only be taken by the verb root. However, in reality, other affixes are possible.

Figure 4: A toy finite-state transducer. A sequence *cook+Past* is translated as *cooked*.

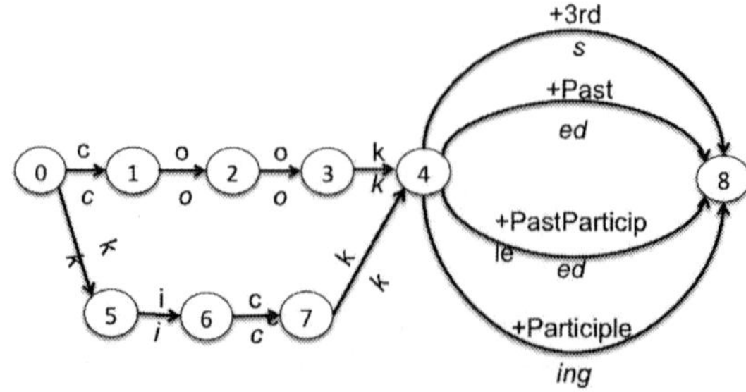

Kawennón:nis is an early-stage research project and only a limited prototype has been released (to a limited audience) and demonstrated to the community. The current version contains 30 verb stems, all bound pronouns and 6 temporal paradigms (Command, Habitual form, Perfective form and Punctual forms which include Definite past, Conditional and Future forms). These were chosen because of their direct and early relevance in the teaching curriculum at Onkwawenna Kentyohkwa. We are working on extending the lexicon to approximately 500 verb roots and including other paradigms.

7   Applications and Evaluation of the Kawennón:nis FST

Because of the early stage of this work and the absence of corpora, Kawennón:nis has not yet been formally evaluated. However, our current workflow involves weekly meetings and consultations with a proficient language speaker, who is a recent graduate of the program and now an educator[10]. The correctness of the rules and the generated forms is checked step-by-step, manually. To the extent possible, we intend to run a statistical evaluation once Kawennón:nis is close to completion.

Currently, the FST model is the backbone of three applications: the web application Kawennón:nis, its mobile app version and a spellchecker. We have already described Kawennón:nis in Section 5. The spellchecker is generated using the Giellatekno infrastructure (Moshagen et al., 2013). The spellchecker only works in Office Libre but it is also unclear if the spellchecker will end up being released or used. There is some hesitance within the community to develop a tool that corrects users' spelling, as there is this approach might be too prescriptive and punitive as well as reinforce a singular dialect, not allowing for minor, but accepted, idiosyncratic differences in spelling. That is to say, just because we *can* develop a particular technology with little extra effort does not necessarily mean we *should*. This question requires further consideration.

Given how time-consuming it is to create a symbolic language model, we intend to use it for as many applications as possible. In the near future, we intend to start a flash-card generator that would allow students learn the subsets of morphology they are most interested in.

The next application we intend to focus on is predictive text on mobile devices.

8   Future Work

In the immediate future we will extend the inventory of verb roots to 500 and work on including all relevant paradigms, namely pre-pronominal prefixes and pre-aspectual suffixes.

It is quite likely that we will be unable to include a majority of derivational affixes because selectional preferences are not uniform across verbs in Kanyen'kéha. This may be addressed to a large extent by subcategorizing the lexicon but this solution may become too unwieldy. In a similar vein, we will probably be unable to properly address noun incorporation due to semantic restrictions. However, we hope to include a small subset of derivational affixes in a held-out, limited set of verbs that will help students master the phenomena of derivational suffixes and noun incorporation.

Although nouns are not as frequent in Kanyen'kéha as verbs, they are obviously still a very important part of the language and thus we will encode some nominal morphology after the verbal part is complete.

One of the biggest problems in collecting a reliable corpus of Kanyen'kéha is dialectal differences. Plans for future work include creating a transducer between dialects which would allow corpora from different dialects to be leveraged and used for statistical learning. It is also our hope that this work be extended to other Iroquoian languages, such as Oneida.

While most of the future work mentioned above is centered around improving the language model, we are also interested in leveraging the generative power of the model by making use of it in other applications. The details will not be clear until Kawennón:nis has been launched and used by the Onkwawenna Kentyohkwa immersion school. That is, what was needed in the initial applications of Kawennón:nis was ascertained by Onkwawenna Kentyohkwa staff who have the perspective that only years of experience can provide, and similarly, future applications and implementations of Kawennón:nis following its initial release will require thoughtful planning and an acute awareness of the needs of Kanyen'kéha teach-

---

[10]This person is the third author of this paper

ers and learners alike. Some potential applications include automatic flash card generators, spellcheckers and predictive text for mobile devices.

9 Conclusions

In this paper we presented preliminary work on Kawennón:nis, a verb conjugator for Kanyen'kéha.

The FST technology behind Kawennón:nis is time-consuming to engineer and difficult to change or adapt, yet the low-data reality of many Indigenous languages is such that we cannot rely on statistical alternatives. In general, smaller languages do not benefit in the short term from recent advances in Language Processing or Machine Learning, due to a general scarcity of linguistic data. Restricting our toolset to newer technologies would preclude us from making progress on this project.

Looking beyond Kawennón:nis, it is important to note the general lack of linguistic software support for most Indigenous languages of North America, with many language communities only recently having their writing systems supported by Unicode or having an input system to write their languages on mobile devices[11] or computers (Pine and Turin, 2018).

With Indigenous languages facing increased pressure from majority languages like English or French, many language activists are turning to technology to assist in reclaiming and revitalizing their languages. Developing basic technological scaffolding to support online communication through social media, text processing tools and reference tools like Kawennón:nis could have an important role to play in this process. It is clear that given the self-determined nature of Indigenous language reclamation efforts that the only way forward is through respectful, contextually-informed collaboration. It is our hope that the development of Kawennón:nis is a small but confident step in the right direction.

Acknowledgements

The authors are grateful Karakwenhawi Zoe Hopkins for allowing the first author to participate in the Kanyen'kéha online course. Many thanks to Antti Arppe and Sjur Moshagen for sharing their experience and for advice on FSTs, and to Jordan Lachler for extensive help on the Linguistics of Iroquoian languages. We are also grateful to Rohahí:yo Jordan Brant and to Ryan DeCaire for patient help with Kanyen'kéha and for multiple suggestions regarding the design of the user interface.

Glossary

CIS - cislocative, DUAL - dualic, FACT - factual, FUT - future, PPFV - past perfective, PUNC - punctual, PURP - purposive, REP - repetitive, REV - reversive, SREFL - semi-reflexive, TRANS - translocative.

References

John Beatly. 1974. *Mohawk Morphology*. Number 2 in Linguistic Series. Museum of Anthropology, University of Northern Colorado, Greeley, Colorado.

Kenneth R. Beesley and Lauri Karttunen. 2003. *Finite State Morphology*. CSLI Publications.

Nancy Bonvillain. 1973. *A Grammar of Akwesasne Mohawk*. Number 8 in Ethnology Division. National Museum of Man, Ottawa, Canada.

Dustin Bowers, Antti Arppe, Jordan Lachler, Sjur Moshagen, and Trond Trosterud. 2017. A morphological parser for Odawa. In *Proceedings of 2nd Workshop on Computational Methods for Endangered Languages (ComputEL-2)*.

Peter Brand, Tracey Herbert, and Shay Boechler. 2015. Language vitalization through online and mobile technologies in british columbia. In Laurel Evelyn Dyson, Stephen Grant, and Max Hendriks, editors, *Indigenous people and mobile technologies*, chapter 17. Routledge.

Karen E. Breiner-Sanders, Pardee Lowe, John Miles, and Elvira Swender. 2000. Actfl proficiency guidelinesspeaking: Revised 1999. *Foreign Language Annals*, 33(1):13–18.

---

[11] With FirstVoices Keyboards and Keyman.

Alain Désilets, Benoit Farley, Geneviève Patenaude, and Marta Stojanovic. 2008. WeBiText: Building large heterogeneous translation memories from parallel web content. *Proc. of Translating and the Computer*, 30:27–28.

Atticus G. Harrigan, Katherine Schmirler, Antti Arppe, Lene Antonsen, Trond Trosterud, and Arok Wolvengrey. 2017. Learning from the computational modelling of Plains Cree verbs. *Morphology*, 27(4):565–598.

Mans Hulden. 2009. Foma: a finite-state compiler and library. In *Proceedings of the 12th Conference of the European Chapter of the Association for Computational Linguistics*, pages 29–32. Association for Computational Linguistics.

Barbara Kelly, Gillian Wigglesworth, Rachel Nordlinger, and Joseph Blythe. 2014. The acquisition of polysynthetic languages. *Language and Linguistics Compass*, 8(2):51–64.

Kimmo Koskenniemi. 1986. Compilation of automata from morphological two-level rules. In F. Karlson, editor, *Papers from the Fifth Scandinavian Conference on Computational Linguistics*, pages 143–149.

Jordan Lachler, Lene Antonsen, Trond Trosterud, Sjur N. Moshagen, and Antti Arppe. 2018. Modeling Northern Haida morphology. In *Proceedings of the Tenth International Conference on Language Resources and Evaluation (LREC 2018)*, May.

Patrick Littell, Aidan Pine, and Henry Davis. 2017. Waldayu and Waldayu Mobile: Modern digital dictionary interfaces for endangered languages. In *Proceedings of the 2nd Workshop on the Use of Computational Methods in the Study of Endangered Languages*, pages 141–150.

Patrick Littell, Anna Kazantseva, Roland Kuhn, Aidan Pine, Antti Arppe, Christopher Cox, and Marie-Odile Junker. forthcoming. Indigenous language technologies in Canada: Assessment, challenges, and successes. *Proceedings from the 27th International Conference on Computational Linguistics*.

Floyd Lounsbury. 1953. *Oneida Verb Morphology*. Yale University Press.

Megan Lukaniec. 2010. Words of the Huron. By John L. Steckley. *International Journal of American Linguistics*, 76(2):304–306.

Brian Maracle. 2017. *Anonymous 1st Year Adult Immersion Program 2017-18*. Onkwawenna Kentyohkwa, Ohsweken, ON, Canada. The book was co-written my several other staff members over the years. Brian Maracle is the author of the latest, 2017 edition.

Joel Martin, Howard Johnson, Benoit Farley, and Anna Maclachlan. 2003. Aligning and using an English-Inuktitut parallel corpus. In *Proceedings of the HLT-NAACL 2003 Workshop on Building and using parallel texts: Data driven machine translation and beyond, Volume 3*, pages 115–118. Association for Computational Linguistics.

Jeffrey Micher. 2017. Improving coverage of an Inuktitut morphological analyzer using a segmental recurrent neural network. In *Proceedings of the 2nd Workshop on the Use of Computational Methods in the Study of Endangered Languages*, pages 101–106. Association for Computational Linguistics.

Marianne Mithun. 1989. The acquisition of polysynthesis. *Journal of Child Language*, 16(2):285–312.

Marianne Mithun. 1996. Grammatical Sketches: the Mohawk Language. In *Quebec's Aboriginal Languages*, pages 159–174. Multilingual Matters Ltd.

Marianne Mithun. 2004. Mohawk and the iroquoian languages. In *Routledge Encyclopedia of Linguistics*. New York: Routledge.

Mehryar Mohri. 1997. Finite-state transducers in language and speech processing. *Computational Linguistics*, 23(2):269–311, June.

Sjur N. Moshagen, Tommi A. Pirinen, and Trond Trosterud. 2013. Building an open-source development infrastructure for language technology projects. In *Proceedings of the 19th Nordic Conference of Computational Linguistics, NODALIDA 2013, May 22-24, 2013, Oslo University, Norway*, pages 343–352.

Aidan Pine and Mark Turin. 2017. Language revitalization. *Oxford Research Encyclopedia of Linguistics*.

Aidan Pine and Mark Turin. 2018. Seeing the heiltsuk orthography from font encoding through to unicode: A case study using convertextract. *3rd Workshop on Collaboration and Computing for Under-Resourced Languages 'Sustaining knowledge diversity in the digital age'*.

Paul M. Postal. 1963. *Some Syntactic Rules in Mohawk*. Ph.D. thesis, Yale University.

Conor Snoek, Dorothy Thunder, Kaidi Lõo, Antti Arppe, Jordan Lachler, Sjur Moshagen, and Trond Trosterud. 2014. Modeling the noun morphology of Plains Cree. In *Proceedings of the 2014 Workshop on the Use of Computational Methods in the Study of Endangered Languages*, pages 34–42, Baltimore, Maryland, USA, June. Association for Computational Linguistics.

TRC. 2015. Truth and Reconciliation Commission of Canada: executive summary. Truth and Reconciliation Commission of Canada, Manitoba: Truth and Reconciliation Commission of Canada.

Using the Nunavut Hansard Data for Experiments in Morphological Analysis and Machine Translation

Jeffrey C. Micher

U.S. Army Research Laboratory
2800 Powder Mill Road
Adelphi, MD 20783
`jeffrey.c.micher.civ@mail.mil`

Abstract

Inuktitut is a polysynthetic language spoken in Northern Canada and is one of the official languages of the Canadian territory of Nunavut. As such, the Nunavut Legislature publishes all of its proceedings in parallel English and Inuktitut. Several parallel English-Inuktitut corpora from these proceedings have been created from these data and are publically available. The corpus used for current experiments is described. Morphological processing of one of these corpora was carried out and details about the processing are provided. Then, the processed corpus was used in morphological analysis and machine translation (MT) experiments. The morphological analysis experiments aimed to improve the coverage of morphological processing of the corpus, and compare an additional experimental condition to previously published results. The machine translation experiments made use of the additional morphologically analyzed word types in a statistical machine translation system designed to translate to and from Inuktitut morphemes. Results are reported and next steps are defined.

1 Introduction

Inuktitut is a polysynthetic language spoken in all areas of Canada north of the treeline, and is one of a group of closely related Inuit languages that includes Inuinnaqtun, Inuvialuktun, Kalaallisut (Greenlandic) and others; there are about 35,000 speakers of these languages in Canada. Inuktitut is of great interest to researchers in machine translation (MT) because it is one of the official languages of a bureaucracy, the government of the Canadian territory of Nunavut, which is continually generating parallel texts: Inuktitut in parallel with English. High-quality MT depends on the existence of large quantities of parallel text that can be used to train MT systems. While its elevated status as an official language has helped to maintain its use, because of the low number of speakers, it has not received a lot of attention by the natural language processing (NLP) research and development community. From a research point of view, the Inuktitut-English language pair is a best-case scenario for people interested in MT into and out of a polysynthetic language. If we eventually succeed in building high-quality Inuktitut-to-English and English-to-Inuktitut MT systems, the lessons learned may be applicable to other language pairs in which one of the languages is polysynthetic. From a **practical** point of view, good Inuktitut-to-English and English-to-Inuktitut MT systems could be used to generate first-draft translations that would make translators working for the Nunavut government more productive, and thus assist the survival and revitalization of the Inuktitut language. Furthermore, NLP tools such as spell checkers or machine translation would greatly benefit speakers of Inuktitut and help to maintain their language by enhancing the speakers' use of the internet or mobile technologies, for example. Because Inuktitut has complex morphology, any such NLP or MT tools will require the development of an accurate morphological analyzer. The purpose of this current line of research is to further develop an existing morphological analyzer, the Uqailaut analyzer, and we report on progress and the use of this work in downstream machine translation experiments.

The structure of this paper is as follows: first, we describe the Inuktitut language in terms of morphological complexity; second, we describe the Nunavut Hansard corpus and the processing that was applied to it; third we describe the existing morphological analyzer, the Uqailaut analyzer; fourth, we

Proceedings of Workshop on Polysynthetic Languages, pages 65–72
Santa Fe, New Mexico, USA, August 20-26, 2018.

present an extension of previous experiments on morphological analysis; fifth, we describe machine translation experiments; finally, we discuss future work envisioned.

2   Background

2.1   The Inuktitut Language

The Inuktitut Language is polysynthetic, and is often used to demonstrate what is meant by polysynthesis. Inuktitut words are very long: they often correspond to what is expressed in a full clause in other languages like English. For example, the two words *Qanniqlaunngikkalauqtuqlu aninngittunga* mean *"Even though it's not snowing a lot, I'm not going out,"* with each word corresponding to one clause in English.

2.2   Inuktitut Word Structure

Inuktitut words generally consist of a root followed by zero or many lexical postbases, followed by a grammatical suffix and possibly a clitic (Dorais, 1990). Lexical postbases can be added recursively, and this is what makes Inuktitut words so long. It is also in the lexical affixes where incorporation is found, with a small set of adjectival and light verb postbases. One of the example words above can be broken into component morphemes as follows:

```
Qanniqlaunngikkalauqtuqlu
qanniq -lak    -uq         -nngit -galauq   -tuq      -lu
snow   -a_little -frequently -NOT   -although -3.IND.S  -and
"And even though it's not snowing alot,"
```

In this example, *qannik* is a root, *lak, uq, nngit, galauq* are lexical postbases, *tuq* is a grammatical suffix, and *lu* is a clitic.

2.3   Inuktitut Morphophonemics

In addition to the ability of roots to be extended with postbases and suffixes, the morphophonemics of Inuktitut are quite complex. Each morpheme in Inuktitut can surface differently depending on its context: this affect its own realization as well as the previous morpheme's realization, and these changes are not phonologically conditioned, but must be learned for each morpheme. As a result, morphological analysis cannot proceed as mere segmentation, but rather, each surface segmentation must map back to an underlying morpheme. In this paper, we refer to these different morpheme forms as 'surface' morphemes and 'deep' morphemes. The example below demonstrates some of the typical morphophonemic alternations that can occur in an Inuktitut word, using the word *mivviliarumalauqturuuq*, 'he said he wanted to go to the landing strip':

```
Romanized Inuktitut word:          mivviliarumalauqturuuq
Surface segmentation     miv -vi    -lia    -ruma -lauq -tu    -ruuq
Deep form segmentation   mit -vik   -liaq   -juma -lauq -juq   -guuq
Gloss                    land -place -go_to -want -PAST -3.IND.S -he_says
```

We proceed from the end to the beginning to explain the morphophonemic rules. The morpheme 'guuq' is a *UVULAR ALTERNATOR*[1], which means the 'g' can be realized as different uvular consonants depending on what precedes it. So 'guuq' changes to 'ruuq' and it also deletes the preceding consonant 'q' of 'juq.' The morpheme 'juq is a *CONSONANT ALTERNATOR*, which means it shows an alternation in its first consonant, which appears as 't' after a consonant, and 'j' otherwise. The morpheme 'lauq' is *NEUTRAL* after a vowel, so there is no change. The morpheme 'juma' is like 'guuq', a uvular alternator, and it deletes. So 'juma' becomes 'ruma,' and the 'q' of the preceding morpheme is deleted. Note, however, how this alternation differs from that found with 'guuq,' be-

---

[1] The names of the various morphophonological processes are those used in (Mallon, 2000) and are not meant to be general terms.

cause the underlying initial phoneme is different. The morpheme 'liaq' is a *DELETER*, so the preceding 'vik' becomes 'vi.' Finally, 'vik' is a VOICER, which causes the preceding 'k' to assimilate completely, so 'mik' becomes 'miv' (Mallon, 2000)[2].

The combination of many morphemes and morphophonemic alternations not phonologically conditioned, makes it absolutely necessary to have a good morphological analyzer for any downstream NLP application. But before looking at the available analyzer, and current experimental results, however, we first discuss the available dataset.

3   The Nunavut Hansard Corpus

The Inuktitut-English corpus, referred to here as the Nunavut Hansard (NH) corpus, originated during the ACL 2003 Workshop entitled "Building and Using Parallel Texts: Data-driven Machine Translation and Beyond[3]," and was made available to researchers during this workshop. The data was subsequently used for a shared task on alignment that took place in the same workshop in 2005[4]. Participants were asked to develop methods of word alignment for this data set, which, at the time, was the only parallel data set containing English and a polysynthetic language, presenting a challenge to the state of the art in word alignment. The dataset was assembled and sentence-aligned, and is described in Martin et al. (2003). The data that was downloaded and used in the experiments described in this paper was version 1.1. Note, the version 1.1 dataset is one file containing a line of Inuktitut, a separator line, a line of English, and another separator line. This dataset was subsequently processed for use in the second workshop mentioned, and provided in the form of three zip files, one containing a "training" set, one a "trial" set, and one, a "test" set[5]. The trial and test sets contained data held out from the training set, and used to develop and test the word alignment algorithms. The data in the training set, however, contained two parallel English and Inuktitut files, and it was these files that were used as the starting point for subsequent pre-processing.

3.1   Corpus Statistics

The corpus that was processed and used in downstream MT experiments contains 340,526 lines of parallel text. The English side contains 3,992,298 tokens, with 27,127 types. The Inuktitut side contains 2,153,034 tokens, with 417,406 types. The type-token ratios of the two data sets are dramatically different: 0.0067 for English vs. 0.1938 for Inuktitut. The percentage of singletons is also dramatically different, with 32.41% in English, vs. 80.93% in Inuktitut. The average word length in characters is: 4.26 in English and 9.31 in Inuktitut. The average line length (number of words in line) is 11.72 in English and 6.22 in Inuktitut.

	English	Inuktitut
Tokens	3,992,298	2,153,034
Types	27,127	417,406
Type-token ratio	0.0067	0.1938
Percentage of singletons	32.41%	80.93%
Average word length in characters	4.26	9.31
Average line length in words	11.72	6.22

Table 1: Nunavut Hansard Corpus Statistics

3.2   Sample Text from the Corpus

The corpus text is typical for legislative proceedings, containing many "Thank you, Mr. Speaker" or "Agreed" lines. As such, the corpus is quite redundant. The most frequent line is "Thank you, Mr.

---

[2] Mallon lists this morpheme as 'mit,' however, the Uqailaut dictionary has 'mik/1 to land or alight after flight' so it appears the Mallon example contains an error.

[3] http://web.eecs.umich.edu/~mihalcea/wpt/

[4] http://www.statmt.org/wpt05/

[5] These files are no longer available. The link to them is broken. However, they can be reconstituted from the original version 1.1 text file

Speaker," appearing approximately 17,000 times. Other than frequently occurring turns of phrase typical of legislative proceedings, the corpus covers various topics germane to the domain of legislature such as taxation, community projects, or committee reports. Below we see some examples of text from the English side of the corpus :

Many of the committees' general observations and comments will be reflected in the reports of the other Standing Committees.

The success of its' implementation depends upon people at all levels of government having a clear understanding of the concept and its' critical importance.

If there are no further questions on the motion, all those in favour to the motion?

I wanted to return to a previous issue in regards to income tax.

Mr. Speaker, decisions surrounding capital projects and which ones were to proceed this year were based on three criteria.

4   Morphological Processing

The current line of research detailed here concerns the processing of morphologically complex languages like Inuktitut for downstream applications such as MT. A crucial step in working with such data is to perform morphological analysis. A hand-made Inuktitut morphological analyzer was developed at the Institute for Information Technology within the National Research Council of Canada (Farley, 2009)[6]. The analyzer was used as downloaded, with no alterations to the source code whatsoever. The analyzer takes an Inuktitut word as input and returns a morphological analysis or multiple morphological analyses if the word is ambiguous. When multiple analyses are returned, they are returned in multiple lines. Each analysis consists of a string of morphemes and related analysis information, enclosed in curly braces, in the form of:

{<surface form>:<deep form>/<morphological analysis information>}{..}{..}..etc.

For example, for the word "maligarmut," meaning "bill, law; something that one follows," in the dative case, the analyzer returns:

{maligar:maligaq/1n}{mut:mut/tn-dat-s}
{mali:malik/1v}{gar:gaq/1vn}{mut:mut/tn-dat-s}

As the analyzer was written in Java, it can be run anywhere. Upon initial investigation of the speed of the analyzer, running it on a standalone laptop, it was determined that certain strategies should be applied to minimize the time spent running the analyzer, since each word analyzed could take anywhere from less than a second to minutes to run. Since the analyzer does not rely on context, we decided to collect up each and every 'type' in the Inuktitut corpus, rather than running the analyzer on each and every 'token': there are a total of 2,153,034 tokens, in the corpus, represented by 417,406 unique types. A database (in multiple file format) of the analyses provided for each word type was created and used in later processing steps to assign the appropriate analysis to each token in the corpus. Types which consisted of alphanumeric characters mixed with numerals, which were often typological processing errors, were filtered out, since these types were shown to fail during morphological processing. As a result, the final number of types for processing was reduced to 413,553. After running the analyzer, there were a total of 287,858 analyzed types, 124,189 types which the analyzer could not process, and a negligible number of types which caused processing errors (1,506).

Comparing to previous work to analyze this corpus with this analyzer, Nicholson et al. (2012) report that the analyzer is able to provide at least a single analysis for approximately 218K Inuktitut types (65%) from the Nunavut Hansard corpus. Their 218K number may be an error, since they report the number of types to be 416K. Nonetheless, their finding that the analyzer does not process each and

---

every type is in line with the current work, with approximately 30% of the types from the corpus not having an analysis.

4.1 Distribution of the Number of Analyses per Type

The number of morphological analyses per type in the Nunavut Hansard corpus varies. The range is from one to 14,596 (for the type, "piliriaksarijattinniittuni"), with a mean of 39.04, a median of nine and a mode of two. So most types have at least two analyses, half of the types have up to nine analyses, and there are some extreme cases.

5 Morphological Analyzer Experiments and Downstream Machine Translation Experiments

The morphological analyses have been used in two sets of downstream experiments, and will be used in continued experiments in this line of research as it progresses.

5.1 Morphological Analyzer Experiments

One set of experiments involved learning a model from the analyzed data to perform morphological analysis of the remaining types which the Uqailaut analyzer could not analyze. Micher (2017) used a segmental recurrent neural network (SRNN) (Kong, Dyer, & Smith, 2015) The results from that work are summarized and presented here for the reader's convenience, and a new experimental condition is reported.

The models in Micher (2017) were trained with approximately 23K types having a single analysis from the Uqailaut analyzer. The reason for using only those with a single analysis is that they can be argued as being the most accurate, according to the Uqailaut analyzer, i.e. there is no ambiguous output to choose from. Inputs to the model are sequences of characters, and outputs are labels with the number of characters that each label covers. Three experimental conditions were designed, reported in (Micher, 2017) and summarized here. The first condition (CG) used coarse-grained output labels (16 total), identifying the general type of morpheme, similar to POS tags. The second (FG) used fine-grained output labels (1691 total) reflecting complete morphological information about each morpheme. The third (FG-SO, "fine-grained, suffixes only") looked at whether the confusion produced by the model could be attributed at least somewhat to the root morphemes, likened to "open-class" vocabulary with high variation, by measuring the precision, recall and F-scores over suffixes alone, with the fine-grained label output. The rational for this experimental condition is the following: root morphemes are similar to "open-class" words in that they represent objects and events. The lexical postbases, grammatical suffixes, and clitics are similar to "closed class" words in that their number is fixed and the category cannot generally increase. There are far fewer suffixes in Inuktitut than roots (potentially unbounded), and for this reason, it was hypothesized that the analyzer would be able to analyze most of the suffixes but perhaps not all of the roots.

Two held out sets (referred to as "dev" and "test", although the "dev" set was merely an additional test set and not used for development purposes) were created. Initially, 1000 items for each set were held out, but because the neural network could not process unseen labels occurring in the two held-out sets, these were reduced to 449 test items each (see (Micher, 2017) for details of the selection process). The two test sets were then run through the model and precision, recall, and F-scores for both segmentation and segmentation+tagging were calculated on the output. These measures are typical in this type of research.

A fourth experimental condition (FG-UNK), not yet published, was devised to address the modeling problem of unseen labels. As is typically currently done in computational modeling of language, data items with fewer than a preselected number of items are replaced with an unknown symbol label (<UNK>) to ensure that all items found in test and development sets are present in training. As such, the <UNK> label was added to the output vocabulary, and the two test sets were resampled, with 1000 items each. Any label in the test sets not appearing in the training data was then changed to <UNK> and the experiments were re-run. Table 2 below summarizes the results from (Micher, 2017) and the new results with <UNK> labels.

As can be seen, the CG output is the best, and this stands to reason, the model only has to decide between 16 labels, versus 1691 (or 1692 labels, in the case of FG-UNK). The FG condition fares worse, only reaching approximately 86% or 83% accuracy in the segmentation only task, and even worse in the segmentation plus tagging task. However, this condition can only fairly be compared to the third condition, FG-SO, in which the test sets are identical. In this case, the accuracy measured on the suffixes only is indeed better than that measured over the full words, which supports the idea that such an analyzer can at least do better on certain parts of the words it's analyzing, the suffixes, because the decision space is smaller and better defined. Indeed, the tagging task, although still lower than the segmentation task, is much improved in FG-SO compared to FG. The fourth condition (FG-UNK) can only fairly be compared to the first condition, CG. We see lower segmentation and tagging scores, but the lower scores are not as dramatically low as in FG and FG-SO, which could partially be attributed to the lower number of test items in these sets. Given that the FG-UNK model is choosing among 1692 labels, as compared to the 16 labels in CG, the lower results should not be interpreted as a disappointment.

model	set	seg/ tag	prec.	recall	f- measure
CG	dev	seg	0.9627	0.9554	0.9591
	1000	tag	0.9602	0.9529	0.9565
	test	seg	0.9463	0.9456	0.9460
	1000	tag	0.9430	0.9424	0.9427
FG	dev	seg	0.8640	0.8647	0.8644
	449	tag	0.7351	0.7357	0.7354
	test	seg	0.8291	0.8450	0.8369
	449	tag	0.7099	0.7235	0.7166
FG-SO	dev	seg	0.8838	0.8860	0.8849
	449	tag	0.8178	0.8199	0.8188
	test	seg	0.8560	0.8807	0.8682
	449	tag	0.7922	0.8151	0.8035
FG-UNK	dev	seg	0.9229	0.9206	0.9218
	1000	tag	0.8649	0.8627	0.8638
	test	seg	0.9169	0.9167	0.9168
	1000	tag	0.8582	0.8581	0.8582

Table 2: SRNN Morphological Analysis Experimental Results : From (Micher, 2017) and new condition, FG-UNK reported

5.2 Downstream Machine Translation Experiments

We report here on a set of machine translation experiments[7] which made use of the morphologically analyzed corpus detailed earlier and the SRNN system details in the previous section. We experimented with statistical machine translation from Inuktitut to English and English to Inuktitut, incorporating the results of the previously discussed neural morphological analyzer, into the Nunavut Hansard corpus for words that do not have an analysis from the Uqailaut analyzer. We used the segmentations obtained from the coarse-grained analyzer previously discussed, as these have the best scores out of all of the conditions examined. We compared three conditions: 1) full Inuktitut words 2) segmented Inuktitut words for those words that the Uqailaut analyzer provided an analysis for, choosing the first analysis provided when multiple analyses are available, and 3) full segmentation, incorporating the segmentation from the SRNN described above for those words not having an analysis. We ran the experiments over two separate divisions of the data into training, dev and test sets, insuring no overlap between train/test or train/dev sets, and we computed statistical significance in each set according to the bootstrap resampling method presented in (Koehn P. , 2004). We used the Moses toolkit (Koehn, et al., 2007) to create the models. We report BLEU scores (Papineni, Roukos, Ward, & Zhu, 2002) for the full word systems, and m-BLEU scores (Luong, Nakov, & Kan, 2010) for the morpheme-based systems. Table 3 displays the results.

---

[7] "Machine Translation for a Low-Resource, Polysynthetic Language" presentation at AMTA, 2016, October 31, 2016. https://amtaweb.org/wp-content/uploads/2016/09/AMTA2016Programv6.html

Set	1a	1b	2a	2b
Direction	IU->EN	EN->IU	IU->EN	EN->IU
Model				
Full Inuktitut words	25.6	14.18	22.74	12.54
Morphed Uqailaut (70%) + nothing	29.43	20.09	28.34	18.39
Morphed Uqailaut (70%) +Neural Morph(30%)	30.35	19.61	*29.85	18.56

Table 3: Statistical Machine Translation to and from English (*denotes statistical significance at p < 0.05)

Admittedly, the results presented in Table 3 are problematic. Upon first glance, it appears that the morphologically analyzed (morphed) Inuktitut systems are all better than the systems that translate full words. However, it should be noted that the morphed scores are m-BLEU scores, whereas those over the full word systems are normal BLEU scores. To make up for this mismatch, we recalculated the m-BLEU scores to yield BLEU scores by rejoining, wherever possible, strings of morphemes back into full words. While these scores do indeed come out higher, they are not shown to be significant, at either the p < 0.05 or p < 0.1 levels. For set 1b, we get a BLEU score of 14.89 with a range of [13.46, 16.33] at 95% confidence and [13.76, 16.11] at 90% confidence, and for set 2b, we get a BLEU score of 13.39, with a range of [12.20, 14.59] at 95% and [12.34, 14.38] at 90%.

We do, however, get at least one significant result (at p < 0.05) when comparing the gains from having more words morphologically analyzed. For set 2a, the 100% morphed 29.85 (95% confidence interval of [28.63, 31.22]) is indeed significant over the 28.34 score from the 70% morphed corpus. However we do not get the same significance for set 1. Both sets 1 and 2 were randomly chosen from the full corpus, avoiding any duplicates between train and test, and tune and test sets. This situation points to significant differences in the two sets of data. Indeed, we built the second set precisely because we did not measure significance on the first set and these results warrant further testing, by building additional sample sets, at a minimum.

6   Future Work

Future work with this morphologically analyzed corpus will entail further work to improve the coverage of morphological analysis, using various neural network architectures ; improving the machine translation results thus far obtained by using alternate neural network architectures ; and increasing the amount of data available for this line of research by processing more of the available Nunavut Hansard data, and making use of the word types with ambiguous analyses.

7   Related Work

There is abundant work on computational approaches to morphological segmentation, and researchers currently are applying neural network models to the problem.. Few researchers, however, have looked at how to map the segmentations obtained to a meaningful unit. Kohonen et al. (2006) map surface segments (allomorphs) to common morphemes (deep morphemes) using character rewrite rules learned automatically for Finnish. However, they only treat roots and not suffixes. To resolve cases of homography rather than collapse allomorphs to common morphemes, Bernhard (2007) examines whether surface forms can be labeled with stem/base, prefix, suffix, or linking element Morphological inflexion generation is investigated in (Faruqui, Tsvetkov, Neubig, & Dyer, 2015), which models a mapping from a base form plus features to a surface form. However, this is the opposite of what we are trying to accomplish here. Specifically for Inuktitut, Johnson and Martin (2003) propose an unsupervised analysis technique which makes use of hubs in an automaton, but they do not carry out experiments with it and report on their findings. No further work on morphological analysis of Inuktitut has been found.

8   Acknowledgments

The author would like to thank the anonymous reviewers for their generous and insightful input into this paper.

Bibliography

Bernhard, D. (2007). Simple Morpheme Labelling in Unsupervised Morpheme Analysis. In C. Peters, V. Jijkoun, T. Mandl, H. Mueller, D. W. Oard, A. Penas, . . . D. Santos (Eds.), *Advances in Multilingual and Multimodal Information Retrieval* (pp. 873-880). Berlin: Springer.

Dorais, L.-J. (1990). The Canadian Inuit and their Language. In D. R. Collins, *Arctic Languages An Awakening* (pp. 185-289). Paris: UNESCO.

Farley, B. (2009). *The Uqailaut Project.* Retrieved from Inuktitut Computing: http://www.inuktitutcomputing.ca/Uqailaut/info.php

Faruqui, M., Tsvetkov, Y., Neubig, G., & Dyer, C. (2015). Morphological Inflection Generation Using Character Sequence to Sequence Learning. Retrieved from http://arxiv.org/abs/1512.06110

Johnson, H., & Martin, J. D. (2003). Unsupervised Learning of Morphology for English and Inuktitut. *HLT-NAACL.*

Koehn, P. (2004). Statistical Significance Tests For Machine Translation Evaluation. *Proceedings of EMNLP 2004* (pp. 388-395). Association for Computational Linguistics.

Koehn, P., Hoang, H., Birch, A., Callison-Burch, C., Federico, M., Bertoldi, N., . . . Herbst, E. (2007). Moses: open source toolkit for statistical machine translation. *Proceedings of the 45th Annual Meeting of the ACL on Interactive Poster and Demonstration Sessions* (pp. 177-180). Stroudsburg, PA, USA: Association for Computational Linguistics.

Kohonen, O., Virpioja, S., & Klami, M. (2006). Allomorfessor: Towards Unsupervised Morpheme Analysis. In C. Peters, T. Deselaers, N. Ferro, J. Gonzalo, G. J. Jones, M. Kurimo, . . . V. Petras (Eds.), *Evaluating Systems for Multilingual and Multimodal Information Access. CLEF 2008.* (pp. 975-982). Berlin: Springer.

Kong, L., Dyer, C., & Smith, N. (2015). Segmental Recurrent Neural Networks. *CoRR.* Retrieved from http://arxiv.org/abs/1511.06018

Luong, M.-T., Nakov, P., & Kan, M.-Y. (2010). A Hybrid Morpheme-word Representation for Machine Translation of Morphologically Rich Languages. *Proceedings of the 2010 Conference on Empirical Methods in Natural Language Processing* (pp. 148-157). Stroudsburg, PA, USA: Association for Computational Linguistics.

Mallon, M. (2000). *Inuktitut Linguistics for Technocrats.* Retrieved from Inuktitut Computing: http://www.inuktitutcomputing.ca/Technocrats/ILFT.php

Micher, J. (2017). Improving Coverage of an Inuktitut Morphological Analyzer Using a Segmental Recurrent Neural Network. *Proceedings of the 2nd Workshop on the Use of Computational Methods in the Study of Endangered Languages* (pp. 101-106). Honolulu, HI: Association for Computational Linguistics.

Nicholson, J., Cohn, T., & Baldwin, T. (2012). Evaluating a Morphological Analyser of Inuktitut. Proceedings of the 2012 Conference of the North American Chapter of the Association for Computational Linguistics: Human Language Technologies (pp. 372-376). Stroudsburg, PA, USA: Association for Computational Linguistics.

Papineni, K., Roukos, S., Ward, T., & Zhu, W.-J. (2002). BLEU: A Method for Automatic Evaluation of Machine Translation. *Proceedings of the 40th Annual Meeting on Association for Computational Linguistics* (pp. 311-318). Stroudsburg, PA, USA: Association for Computational Linguistics.

Lost in Translation: Analysis of Information Loss During Machine Translation Between Polysynthetic and Fusional Languages

Manuel Mager[1], Elisabeth Mager[2],
Alfonso Medina-Urrea[3], Ivan Meza[1], Katharina Kann[4]

[1]Instituto de Investigaciones en Matemáticas Aplicadas y en Sistemas,
Universidad Nacional Autónoma de México, México
[2]Facultad de Estudios Superiores Acatlán, Universidad Nacional Autónoma de México, México
[3]Centro de Estudios Lingüísticos y Literarios, El Colegio de México, México
[4]Center for Data Science, New York University, USA
`mmager@turing.iimas.unam.mx`

Abstract

Machine translation from polysynthetic to fusional languages is a challenging task, which gets further complicated by the limited amount of parallel text available. Thus, translation performance is far from the state of the art for high-resource and more intensively studied language pairs. To shed light on the phenomena which hamper automatic translation to and from polysynthetic languages, we study translations from three low resource, polysynthetic languages (Nahuatl, Wixarika and Yorem Nokki) into Spanish and vice versa. Doing so, we find that in a morpheme-to-morpheme alignment an important amount of information contained in polysynthetic morphemes has no Spanish counterpart, and its translation is often omitted. We further conduct a qualitative analysis and, thus, identify morpheme types that are commonly hard to align or ignored in the translation process.

1 Introduction

Until a few years ago, research on machine translation (MT) between polysynthetic and fusional languages did not get much attention from the natural language processing (NLP) community. Furthermore, with the rise of neural MT (NMT), the common assumption that machine learning approaches for MT were language independent routed the efforts into the direction of general model improvements. But this assumption does not hold completely true, and, recently, efforts have been made to adapt models to individual languages, e.g., in order to improve poor results on morphologically-rich languages (Ataman and Federico, 2018; Al-Mannai et al., 2014; Lee et al., 2016). Koehn (2005) mentioned this problem while he analyzed the Europarl corpus, stating that "translating from an information-rich into an information-poor language is easier than the other way around". However, doing so, we unfortunately note a loss of information. This idea that some languages encode more information in one phrase than others given rise to many questions in linguistics and NLP, and motivated this paper. Polysynthetic languages are a special type of information-rich languages, and come with their own set of challenges for translation. Studying their particularities is an important prerequisite to enable successful translation to or from them in the future.

Many polysynthetic languages—many of which endangered—are spoken in regions where Spanish, English, or Portuguese are dominant. Thus, improving the translation quality of MT between fusional and polysynthetic languages might play an important role for communities which speak a polysynthetic language, e.g., by making documents in key fields such as legal, health and education accessible to them. Although many members of these communities can obtain access to this information using another dominant language which they also speak, this situation might have a negative effect on their native languages due to them not playing a functional role in day-to-day interaction about these important fields. As a result, these dominated languages might be perceived as less important. Well-performing

Proceedings of Workshop on Polysynthetic Languages, pages 73–83
Santa Fe, New Mexico, USA, August 20-26, 2018.

MT might offer the mechanism to invert this situation, by making important documents accessible to the communities in their native languages, thus mitigating the need to consider one language more important, since both allow access to the same sets of documents. Rule-based MT (RBMT) has been a common approach to deal with low-resource MT. However, statistical MT (SMT) and NMT are essential for a broad coverage, due to the vast diversity of polysynthetic languages.

In this paper, we introduce the following research questions: (i) Which information is commonly not encoded in the target text when translating to a fusional language from a polysynthetic one? (ii) How can this information loss be explained from a linguistic point of view? (iii) Are some morphemes particularly hard to translate?

In an attempt to start answering the before mentioned questions, we present a quantitative study, using morpheme-based SMT alignments (Brown et al., 1993) between the following language pairs: Nahuatl-Spanish, Wixarika-Spanish, and Yorem Nokki-Spanish[1]. With the exception of Spanish, all these languages are from the Yuto-Nahua linguistic family and have different levels of polysynthesis. We search for commonly not aligned morphemes and analyze the results. Trying to find answers to our research questions, we also present the qualitative aspects of this information loss.

2   About Polysynthetic Languages

Translating from a polysynthetic language to a fusional one faces difficulties; a significant number of morphemes can get lost because polysynthetic languages have structures that are different from those of fusional languages. A main difference between the fusional and the polysynthetic languages lays at the syntax level of a sentence. Johanna Nichols refers to a binary system, "directed relations between a head and a dependent" (Nichols, 1986), between a head-marked and a dependent-marked relation. While the dependent-marked sentence is characterized by a relation of dependent pronoun-noun and relative construction, the head-marked construction prefers governed arguments, possessed noun, main-clause predicate and inner and outer adverbial constructions. For her "the head is the word which governs, or is subcategorized for –or otherwise determines the possibility of occurrence of– the other word. It determines the category of its phrase." In contrast of the most Indo-European languages, "the Mayan, Athabaskan, Wakashan, Salishan, Iroquoian, Siouan, and Algonkian families are consistently head-marking" (Nichols, 1986), among others. So the polysynthetic languages prefer a head-marked morphology, where the verb has a preference position; "the verb itself normally constitutes a complete sentence; full NP's are included only for emphasis, focus, disambiguation etc." (Nichols, 1986).

In the same way, Baker distinguishes "head-marking" languages from "dependent-marking" ones (Baker, 1996). The first type of languages, in the most cases, has a "head-final structure (SOV)" or a free word order, while the second type exhibits a head-initial structure (SVO or VSO) (Baker, 1996). We must note that not all polysynthetic languages have the head-final structure, for example in Nahuatl we also find an SVO structure as we will see in §6. Jeff MacSwan pointed out that in Southeast Puebla Nahuatl we can find different structures, depending the meaning of each sentence: the SVO-structure is the most natural, the VSO-structure is employed for focus and contrast only and the SOV-structure for light emphasis, but is "also possible for focus or contrast" (MacSwan, 1998). In contrast, in Wixarika the SOV-structure dominates, which makes it less flexible that Nahuatl. The same phenomenon can also be observed in fusional languages. While English prefers an SVO-structure, in German different orders are possible: we can find the SOV-structure only in subordinate sentences, while in main sentences we can have either an SVO-structure, or an OVS-structure for emphasis. In contrast, in Nahuatl the OVS-structure is unacceptable (MacSwan, 1998).

Baker states "that in a polysynthetic language like Mohawk, all verbs necessarily agree with subjects, objects, and indirect objects, except for the special case when the direct object is incorporated into the verb" (Baker, 1996). So "every argument of a head element must be related to a morpheme in the word containing that head (an agreement morpheme, or an incorporated root)" (Baker, 1996), often expressed

---

[1]The language we call Wixarika is also known as Huichol, and Yorem Nokki is also known as Mayo or Yaqui. Similarly, the Yuto-Nahua linguistic family also goes by the name of Uto-Aztec. We use these names out of respect to the communities that have chosen these names within the language.

by asserts. José Luis Iturrioz and Paula Gómez López observe a semantic relation between the predicate and the arguments. For this reason, the enunciative functions as a perspective or situation, individuation, or identification (attribution, reference), discursive cohesion, culminating in the integration of one clause in another (Iturrioz Leza and López Gómez, 2006). This phenomenon cannot be observed in fusional languages; thus, morphemes with specific incorporation functions do not exist in fusional languages. Therefore translation of such kind of morphemes can be challenging in the machine translation process. Moreover, it can be difficult for these morphemes to be inferred when the target language is a polysynthetic one.

Incorporation is a common phenomenon in polysynthetic languages. Wilhelm von Humboldt first described it. For him, incorporation has a syntactical, but not a morphological function (Iturrioz Leza and López Gómez, 2006). In contrast, Marianne Mithun referred to noun incorporation (NI) (Mithun, 1986) in the context of verb morphology. For her "New topics may be introduced in other ways, however IN's do, on occasion, serve to introduce new topics – simply because they are parts of complex verbs denoting conceptually unitary activities" (Mithun, 1986). Also, the NI is not simply a combination of a noun with a verb stem "to yield a more specific, derived verb stem" (Mithun, 1986). According to Baker's theory of incorporation, in polysynthetic languages there exists an interrelation of morphemes, in the way "that one part of a derived stem is the syntactic complement of the other part. In both cases, syntactic argument relationships are being expressed morphologically" (Baker, 1996). Then, we have agreement morphemes, expressing the argument of the verb, e.g., pronominal affixes and incorporated roots (Baker, 1996). "The word-internal structure in these languages is very configurational indeed (...) the order of basic morphemes is also quite consistent (...) Furthermore, (...) this morpheme order provides a clue to the basic syntactic structure of these languages" (Baker, 1996).

One important property of polysynthetic languages is the high number of morphemes which often occur in the verb structure. According to Paula Gómez, in the Wixarika language there are three positions before the verb stem for approximately twelve prefixes, which correspond to different senses; for example, expression of localization, individuation, participation, aspects and modes of action, among others (Gómez, 1999). Like Nichols, his phenomenon of three-place verbs we observe also in the Bantu and Mayan languages (Nichols, 1986). Hence, a considerable number of words, encoding a significant amount of information, may be produced when combining these items. In polysynthetic languages, there is a higher fragmentation of words and an interrelation of the morphemes, making their translation more difficult. Nichols mentions that "in a number of North American families (Uto-Aztecan, Yuman, Pomoan, Siouan, Algonkian, Cadoan), instrumental, locative, and directional affixes on verbs are grammaticalized" (Nichols, 1986). Besides, the morphology of the Wixarika verbs presents complications due to the great number of positions of affixes, which can reach to 20 morphemes or more, forming a morphological chain (Gómez, 1999). Also, in Wixarika, the spatial or local relationships are expressed by adverbs, postpositions, nominal suffixes, and verbal prefixes (Gómez, 1999). For this reason, in many cases, we do not have a correlation of structures in a pair consisting of a polysynthetic and a fusional language, which can make translating difficult. In languages like Spanish, this information is commonly inferred or not encoded in the translation between languages of these two typologies. For instance, consider the Wixarika morpheme "u" that indicates that an action happens in the visual sphere of the speaker. This information is usually not directly translated to Spanish. However, as a result, a problem arises when trying to translate such a phrase back to Wixarika, because the information if the action is held in the visual field of the speaker or not is not available.

3 Previous Work

Nowadays, the area of NLP is largely dominated by data-driven—often neural—approaches which, as far as the machine learning model is concerned, strive to be language-independent. However, the performance of such systems does still vary in dependence of the typology of each language. In order to shed light on this phenomenon and its causes, Cotterell et al. (2018) studied how the difficulty of language modeling (LM) depends on the language. They found inflectional morphology to be a key factor: even character-based long short-term memory (LSTM) models performed worse for morphologically rich languages. In this paper, we will study the causes of possible performance loss for polysynthetic languages in MT.

MT has made a big step forward with the development of SMT and, later on, NMT. Those approaches make it possible to construct reasonably well performing MT systems using parallel corpora that can be gathered from a wide range of sources, and do not need handwritten rules generated by experts. This is crucial, due to the large number of polysynthetic languages. However, most systems fail to achieve good performances for polysynthetic languages, particularly in a low-resource context; with often better results for SMT than for NMT (Mager and Meza, 2018). In recent years, character-based NMT systems were claimed to handle sub-word phenomena (Sennrich et al., 2016), and others target specifically morpho-logical rich languages (Passban et al., 2018; Peyman et al., 2018), but with the condition of feeding the neural network with vast amounts of data. Character-based NMT systems can learn some morphological aspects (Belinkov et al., 2017) even for morphologically rich languages like Arabic. Vania and Lopez (2017) analyzed this proposal, concluding that, although character-based models improve translation, best results are achieved with accurate morphological segmentation.

The problem exposed in this paper has mainly been studied in the context of SMT approaches. This line of research has pursued both the goal of improving translation from morphologically-rich languages into morphologically-poorer ones like English (Habash and Sadat, 2006), and the other way around (Avramidis and Koehn, 2008; Oflazer, 2008). One important development was the inclusion of linguistic markups into factored translation models (Koehn and Hoang, 2007; Oflazer, 2008; Fraser, 2009). Vir-pioja et al. (2007) proposed a combined usage of Morfessor (Creutz and Lagus, 2005), an unsupervised segmentation model, and phrase-based SMT systems, in order to make use of segmented input. The translation improvement through initial morphological segmentation was also found for translation of the polysynthetic Wixarika into Spanish (Mager Hois et al., 2016). In each case the main goal of previous work was to increase the BLEU score. However, in this paper we aim to improve our understanding of the information which is lost in the translation process; and particularly for polysynthetic languages. For this, we make use of morphological segmentation.

4 Morpheme Alignment Between a Polysynthetic and a Fusional Language

Morphemes are the smallest meaning-bearing units of words. Here, we want to know why some of them are not aligned correctly by common SMT systems. We use the surface form of morphemes obtained from manually segmented words in each language and apply the IBM models 2, 3 and 4 (Brown et al., 1993) to get alignment cepts for each morpheme. Each cept contains a (possibly empty) set of positions with which a token is aligned. Also a special cept is defined, that is aligned to morphemes that could not be aligned to any other cept, and is referred to with number 0. A set of alignments is denoted by $A(e, f)$, where f is a phrase of size m in a source language and e is a phrase of size l in a target language.

For our experiments, we use the resulting alignment function obtained from the training process which consists of maximizing the translation likelihood of the training set. The probability of a translation f in the target language, given a source sentence e, is then calculated as:

$$Pr(f|e) = \sum_a Pr(f, a|e) \tag{1}$$

The alignments $a \in A$ are trained jointly with the whole translation model, as defined by Brown et al. (1993). The underlined conditional probability a in Equation 2 is what we use for our work.

$$Pr(f, a|e) = P(m|e) \prod_{j=1}^{m} \underbrace{Pr(a_j|a_1^{j-1}, f_1^{j-1}, m, e)}_{a} Pr(f_j|a_1^{j}, f_1^{j-1}, m, e) \tag{2}$$

After computing the alignments for each sentence pair in our dataset, we count all morphemes which are not aligned, in order to find information that is not expressed in the target language. As SMT is a probabilistic method the resulting alienations are not exact and should be taken as an approximation. Adding this fact, also the amount of data used to train the system influences the resulting inference.

5 Experiments

In order to get the alignments of morphemes in Nahuatl, Wixarika and Yorem Nokki with their Spanish counterparts, we train a word-based SMT system using GIZA++ (Och and Ney, 2003) on parallel datasets in the respective languages, which we will describe below. We parsed the resulting alignment files to extract non-aligned morphemes in each translation direction. As we are working with three language pairs and are interested in both translation directions, we trained six models (Spanish-Wixarika, Wixarika-Spanish, Spanish-Nahuatl, Nahuatl-Spanish, Spanish-Yorem Nokki and Yorem Nokki-Spanish).

5.1 Languages

Nahuatl is a language of the Yuto-Nahua language family and the most spoken native language in Mexico. The variants of this language are diverse, and in some cases can be considered linguistic subgroups. Its almost $1,700$ thousand native speakers mainly live in Puebla, Guerrero, Hidalgo, Veracruz, and San Luis Potosi, but also in Oaxaca, Durango, Modelos, Mexico City, Tlaxcala, Michoacan, Nayarit and the State of Mexico. In this work we use the Northern Puebla variant.

Like all languages of the Yuto-Nahua family, Nahuatl is agglutinative, and a word can consist of a combination of many different morphemes. In contrast to other languages, Nahuatl has a preference for SVO, but SOV and VSO are also used. An example phrase is:

ka-te   ome   no-kni-wan
is-pl.   two   pos.1sg:s.-brother-pl.
I have two brothers

This Nahuatl variant has five vowels ($\{i, u, e, o, a\}$) and does not distinguish if they are short or large. The alphabet of Nahuatl consists of 17 symbols: $\Sigma_{Nahuatl} = \{a,e,h,i,k,m,n,o,p,r,s,t,u,w,x,y,'\}$.

Wixarika is a language spoken by approximately fifty thousand people in the Mexican states of Jalisco, Nayarit, Durango and Zacatecas. It belongs to the Coracholan group of languages within the Yuto-Nahua family. Its alphabet consists of 17 symbols ($\Sigma_{Wixarika}=\{\,',a,e,h,i,+,k,m,n,p,r,t,s,u,w,x,y\}$), out of which five are vowels $\{a,e,i,u,+\}^2$ with long and short variants. An example for a phrase in the language is:

yu-huta-me   ne-p+-we-'iwa
an-two-ns   1sg:s-asi-2pl:o-brother
I have two brothers

This language has a strong SOV syntax, with heavy agglutination on the verb. Wixarika is considered morphologically more complex than other languages from the same family (Iturrioz Leza and López Gómez, 2006).

Yorem Nokki is part of the Taracachita subgroup of the Yuto-Nuahuan language family. Its Southern dialect (commonly known as Mayo) is spoken by close to fifty thousand people in the Mexican states of Sinaloa and Durango, while its Northern dialect (also known as Yaqui) has about forty thousand speakers in the Mexican state of Sonora. In this work, we consider the Mayo dialect. As in the other studied languages, the nominal morphology of Yorem Nokki is rather simple, but, again, the verb is highly complex. Yorem Nokki uses mostly SOV.

The symbols used in our dataset are $\Sigma_{YoremNokki}=\{á,k,s,g,ó,j,y,w,\beta,p,m,e,n,d,r,é,t,u,c,o,h,f,b,',i,l,a\}$, with 8 being vowels: $\{a,e,i,o,u,á,é,ó\}$. An example phrase is:

woori   saila-m-ne   hipu-re
two   brother-pl.-me   have-r
I have two brothers

---

[2]While linguists often use a dashed i (ɨ) to denote the last vowel, in practice almost all native speakers use a plus symbol (+). In this work, we chose to use the latter.

5.2 Dataset

To create our datasets, we use phrases in the indigenous languages paired with their Spanish equivalents. Namely, our translations are taken from books of the collection *Archive of Indigenous Languages* for Nahuatl (Lastra de Suárez, 1980), Wixarika (Gómez, 1999), and Yorem Nokki (Freeze, 1989). A total of 594 phrases is available for each language. To obtain these phrases, a questionnaire of 594 utterances made by Ray Freeze was used (Freeze, 1989, p. 15). In essence, each author elicited equivalent expressions from speakers of the target language. Also, the uniformity of the questionnaire may have been modified because of cultural or environmental circumstances. In cases where the expression could not be elicited, a sentence was offered as similar as possible, grammatically and semantically, to the original utterance. In this manner, the sets of expressions are equivalent for all languages, so we can directly compare results. The words of the polysynthetic languages have already been segmented by linguists in the cited books. In order to achieve a morpheme-to-morpheme translation (instead of a word-to-morpheme one) we segment the Spanish phrases with Morfessor (Virpioja et al., 2013) and manually correct segmentation errors.

5.3 Results and Discussion

Table 1 shows the top fifteen non-aligned morphemes resulting from translating Nahuatl, Wixarika, and Yorem Nokki into Spanish. Naturally, it would be interesting to discuss the syntax of all morphemes in detail. In this way it could be established, for example, what kinds of markers are more characteristic of which kind of language. However, this is out-of-scope for this work, such that we will limit ourselves to the following remarks.

For Wixarika we can see that the eight morphemes which are most challenging for translation are sub-word units. The important Wixarika independent asserters "p+" and "p" are the most frequent morphemes in this language. However, as they have no direct equivalent in Spanish, their translation is mostly ignored. The same is true for the object agreement morphemes "a" and "ne". This is particularly problematic for the translation in the other direction, i.e., from Spanish into Wixarika, as a translator has no information about how the target language should realize such constructions. Human translators can, in some cases, infer the missing information. However, without context it is generally complicated to get the right translation. Also, other morphemes like "u", "e", and "r" encode precise information about forms and movement that are not usually expressed in Spanish. Some of the other morphemes for which the alignment fails, like "ne" and "ti", could have been translated as a first person possessive, or as a question mark, respectively. The reason for those errors might be our low-resource setting.

The Yorem Nokki suffixes "k" and "ka" are realization morphemes. As this construction is not commonly expressed in a fusional or isolating language, it will frequently not be aligned with any Spanish token. Another difficulty is the translation of a concatenative word construction into a fusional one. Yorem Nokki does not use as many agreement morphemes as Wixarika or Nahuatl, but the "si" noun agreement morpheme still is one of the hardest to align. The morpheme "ta" represents the accusative verbal case that can be expressed in Spanish, but still appears as one of the most difficult morphemes to align. This can be a consequence of the low-resource setting we have.

The last language pair (Nahuatl-Spanish) has less non-aligned morphemes than the previews ones. Nahuatl is also the only language for which the most frequently unaligned token is a word: the token "in" is an article. However, its translation is not trivial. As most Yuto-Nahua languages, Nahuatl does not mark grammatical gender (Mager Hois, 2017). The lack of gender information can hurt SMT performance. In practice, for such cases post-processing can be used to correct some of the system errors (Stymne, 2011). However, as in the previous cases, the object ("k" and "ki") a noun agreement morphemes ("ni" and "ti") are the most frequently unaligned morphemes.

Table 2 shows the amount of non-aligned tokens, words, and morphemes for each language pair and each translation direction. Our first observation is that the rate of non-aligned tokens for the direction Spanish-polysynthetic language is far lower than the other way around. The highest rates of non-aligned tokens are found for Wixarika and Yorem Nokki with 0.617 and 0.616, respectively. For Nahuatl and Spanish, this rate is with 0.448 notably lower. On the other hand, the translation direction from Spanish

Wixarika - Spanish				Spanish - Wixarika			
Token	**Alig**	**Non**	**Diff**	**Token**	**Alig**	**Non**	**Diff**
p+-	4	294	-290	el	13	119	-106
ne-	34	208	-174	de	13	81	-68
ti-	3	162	-159	-s	33	86	-53
p-	24	153	-129	en	7	58	-51
u-	2	102	-100	¿	8	47	-39
a-	7	106	-99	la	22	61	-39
e-	3	74	-71	que	27	52	-25
r-	9	73	-64	a	46	65	-19
eu-	2	64	-62	!	5	19	-14
t+a	3	54	-51	con	5	19	-14
k+	1	47	-46	lo	6	17	-11
ta-	9	52	-43	?	24	33	-9
m+-	6	43	-37	ó	5	13	-8
'u-	3	37	-34	és	0	6	-6
ye-	12	44	-32	casa	11	17	-6

Yorem Nokki - Spanish				Spanish - Yorem Nokki			
Token	**Alig**	**Non**	**Diff**	**Token**	**Alig**	**Non**	**Diff**
-k	1	185	-184	está	6	37	-31
-ka	25	143	-118	?	11	32	-21
ta	8	88	-80	la	32	48	-16
ne	40	114	-74	con	7	17	-10
si	1	58	-57	para	4	13	-9
e'	7	62	-55	que	33	41	8
wa	1	54	-53	va	5	13	-8
wa-	2	55	-53	-ndo	1	9	-8
a	25	72	-47	al	8	16	-8
ka-	6	52	-46	se	25	33	-8
wi	7	49	-42	un	1	8	-7
a'	5	46	-41	yo	7	12	-5
po	36	73	-37	las	3	8	-5
βa	3	37	-37	están	3	8	-5
ta-	5	35	-30	ustedes	3	8	-5

Nahuatl - Spanish				Spanish - Nahuatl			
Token	**Alig**	**Non**	**Diff**	**Token**	**Alig**	**Non**	**Diff**
o-	25	214	-189	-a	10	95	-85
in	77	222	-145	-s	30	82	-52
-tl	2	108	-106	?	6	45	-39
ni-	9	111	-102	es	18	45	-27
i	23	73	-50	de	32	55	-23
k-	6	54	-48	!	3	21	-18
ki-	11	54	-43	que	29	45	-16
ti-	13	56	-43	¿	17	32	-15
mo-	16	54	-38	está	15	22	-7
n-	2	40	-38	-o	1	7	-6
k	10	37	-27	-do	3	8	-5
'ke	5	29	-24	-n	1	6	-5
te	3	25	-22	con	10	14	-4
ka-	10	29	-19	están	2	6	-4
-to	4	22	-22	-ra	0	4	-4

Table 1: Alignment results between language pairs. The *Token* column stands for a word or morpheme (morphemes contains the - symbol), *Alig* is the number of times that the token was aligned, *Non* is the number of times the token was not aligned, and *Diff* is the difference between the numbers of aligned and non-aligned tokens.

to our polysynthetic languages seems to work much better and shows less variability. The lowest rate is obtained for Yorem Nokki with 0.264, followed by Nahuatl with 0.277, and Wixarika with 0.35. For both directions, translation with Wixarika got the highest non-alignment rates. This suggests that the phenomenon might be related to the number of morphemes per word: Kann et al. (2018) showed that Wixarika has the highest morphemes-per-word rate among the languages considered here.

To sum up, some fine-grained information from verbs in our polysynthetic languages are not usually

	Tokens	N.a. Tokens	N.a. words	N.a. morph.	N.a./tokens
Wixarika-Spanish	4702	2905	790	2115	0.617
Spanish-Wixarika	3594	1259	1259	0	0.350
Nahuatl-Spanish	4391	1969	1111	858	0.448
Spanish-Nahuatl	3380	939	939	0	0.277
Yorem Nokki-Spanish	4805	2960	2238	722	0.616
Spanish-Yorem Nokki	3163	836	836	0	0.264

Table 2: Alignments of tokens, words, morphemes and their success rates for all language pairs. *N.a. Tokens* counts all non-aligned tokes, *N.a. words* counts only non-aligned words (one morpheme per token), *N.a. morph.* are the non-aligned morphemes. *N.a./tokens* is the rate of non-aligned tokens in relation to the total number of tokens.

translated to Spanish, since this information is not commonly expressed in this target languages. It is particularly true for structure morphemes and agreement morphemes, as well as enunciation functions (situations, individuation, attribution, reference, and discursive cohesion).

The severity of the alignment problem seems to correlate with the BLEU metric for translation of these language pairs (Mager and Meza, 2018): translation from polysynthetic languages to fusional ones has been reported to work notably better than the opposite direction. We expect the alignment issue to be fundamental for explaining this dynamic.

6   Information Loss in Translation Between Polysynthetic and Fusional Languages

As discussed in §5, an important amount of morphemes from a polysynthetic language usually will often not be aligned to morphemes of an fusional language. However, how can we explain such a loss of information? In this section, we will conduct a qualitative analysis to obtain a better understanding of this phenomenon.

Namely, we will analyze the phrase "She always asks us for tortillas." in our three polysynthetic languages. The first example, taken from Gómez (1999), will be in Wixarika:

m+k+	pa:pa	ya	p+-ta-ti-u-ti-wawi-ri-wa
Ella	tortilla	enf	asi-1pl:o-its-vis-pl:a-pedir-apl-hab

Free Spanish translation: Ella siempre nos pide tortillas
Free English translation: She always asks us for tortillas
Abbreviations:

enf	empathic
asi	independent asserter
pl:o	plural of the indirect object
its	intensifier
vis	visible: in the ambit of the speaker
pl:a	plurality of the action
appl	applicative
hab	habitual

Wixarika employs a head-final structure (SOV) as can be seen in the example. Therefore, we have in the third place the emphatic factor "ya" which realizes the agreement of the initial subject and the direct object; also we need an asserter for the indirect object "ta", what in this case is the morpheme "p+", which we cannot translate. In fact, "p+" was the most unaligned morpheme in table 1. The verb exists of different prefixes collocated before the verb stem "wawi": the morpheme "ti" is an intensifier of the visibility of the ambit of the speaker, expressed with the morpheme "u"; the prefix "ti" on the first place of the verb refers to the plurality of the action and the plural of the direct object. Therefore, we can speak of an incorporation of the object into the verb. All these prefixes cannot be directly translated.

Next, we analyze our example phrase in the Nahuatl Acaxochitlan dialect, spoken in Hidalgo (Lastra de Suárez, 1980), and its translation into Spanish:

ye'wa	tech-tla-tlanilia	semian	in-tlaxkal-i
ella	1pl.obj-indef-pide	siempre	art-tortilla-abs

	Free Spanish translation:	Ella siempre nos pide tortillas
	Free English translation:	She always asks us for tortillas
	Abbreviations:	
	abs	absolutive
	art	article
	indef	indefinite
	obj	object
	pl	plural

In the Nahuatl language we also see a loss of information, but less than in Wixarika. Here, we notice a different syntactic structure: the direct object is located at the end of the phrase and the indirect object is located in the second place. Thus, we have an SOVO structure. What is not translated is the prefix "ya" of the verb "yanilia" (ask for) because the undefined situation of an action is unknown in the fusional languages, as well as the absolutive suffix "i" of the object "tlaxkal" (tortillas)

Finally, we consider the same example for Yorem Nokki, taken from the Mayo dialect of Yorem Nokki (Southern branch), which is spoken in the Mexican state of Sinaloa (Freeze, 1989):

hiβa	a:po	tahkari-m	ito-wi	a'a:wa
siempre	ella	ortilla-pl	nosotros-a	hab-pide
Free Spanish translation:		Ella siempre nos pide tortillas		
Free English translation:		She always asks us for tortillas		
Abbreviations:				
		hab	habitual	
		pl	plural	

In the Yorem Nokki language, we have a head final structure (SOV) like in Wixarika. However this phrase has only one morpheme that cannot be directly translated to Spanish, e.g., the prefix "a" that expresses an habitual action.

7   Conclusion and Future Work

We presented a quantitative and a qualitative study of the information loss that occurs during MT from three polysynthetic languages of the Yuto-Nahua family into Spanish, a fusional language, and vice versa. Based on GIZA++ alignments between Spanish morphemes and the corresponding morphemes in our polysynthetic languages, we got insight into which morphemes are commonly not translated. We found that, in contrast to the morphemes in the polysynthetic languages, most Spanish tokens get aligned by the aligner.

We further noticed that often fine-grained information which is encoded into polysynthetic verbs is not translated, since this information is not commonly expressed in our fusional language. The same holds true for polysynthetic structure morphemes and agreement morphemes. Other morphemes which are hard to translate are the enunciation functions, like perspectives or situations, individuation, attribution, reference, and discursive cohesion. In Wixarika, the hardest morphemes to translate are the assignors "p+", "p" and "m+", the object agreement morphemes "a" and "ne", and the action perspective morphemes "u" and "e"; for Yorem Nokki the realization morphemes "ka" and "k" and the "si" noun agreement morpheme; for Nahuatl the object agreement morphemes like "k" and "ki" and the noun agreement morphemes "ni" and "ti". By revision of non-aligned morphemes we could also see that our three analyzed polysynthetic languages have entirely different structures, but in all cases, the agreement morphemes represented were hard to align with Spanish morphemes.

In future work, we aim to increase the amount of data to train our MT models. For instance, with the usage of automatic morphological segmentation systems like the one presented by Kann et al. (2018), we could use larger amounts of parallel data for training and, thus, reduce alignment errors in our experiments. Such an error reduction for alignments could help us to identify in a cleaner way the underlying phenomena that hurt MT for the languages considered here.

Acknowledgments

We would like to thank all the anonymous reviewers for their valuable comments and feedback.

References

Kamla Al-Mannai, Hassan Sajjad, Alaa Khader, Fahad Al Obaidli, Preslav Nakov, and Stephan Vogel. 2014. Unsupervised word segmentation improves dialectal arabic to english machine translation. In *Proceedings of the ANLP*, pages 207–216.

Duygu Ataman and Marcello Federico. 2018. Compositional representation of morphologically-rich input for neural machine translation. *arXiv preprint arXiv:1805.02036*.

Eleftherios Avramidis and Philipp Koehn. 2008. Enriching morphologically poor languages for statistical machine translation. *Proceedings of 2008 Anual Meeting of ACL*, pages 763–770.

Mark C Baker. 1996. *The polysynthesis parameter*. Oxford University Press.

Yonatan Belinkov, Nadir Durrani, Fahim Dalvi, Hassan Sajjad, and James Glass. 2017. What do neural machine translation models learn about morphology? In *Proceedings of the 2017 Annual Meeting of the ACL*, volume 1, pages 861–872.

Peter F Brown, Vincent J Della Pietra, Stephen A Della Pietra, and Robert L Mercer. 1993. The mathematics of statistical machine translation: Parameter estimation. *Computational linguistics*, 19(2):263–311.

Ryan Cotterell, Sebastian J. Mielke, Jason Eisner, and Brian Roark. 2018. Are all languages equally hard to language-model? In *Proceedings of the 2018 Conference of the NAACL-HLT*, New Orleans, June.

Mathias Creutz and Krista Lagus. 2005. *Unsupervised morpheme segmentation and morphology induction from text corpora using Morfessor 1.0*. Helsinki University of Technology Helsinki.

Alexander Fraser. 2009. Experiments in morphosyntactic processing for translating to and from german. In *Proceedings of the Fourth WMT*, pages 115–119. Association for Computational Linguistics.

Ray A Freeze. 1989. Mayo de Los Capomos, Sinaloa. In *Archivos de lenguas indígenas de México*, volume 14. El Colegio de México.

Paula Gómez. 1999. Huichol de San Andrés Cohamiata, Jalisco. In *Archivos de lenguas indígenas de México*, volume 22. El Colegio de México.

Nizar Habash and Fatiha Sadat. 2006. Arabic preprocessing schemes for statistical machine translation. In *Proceedings of the 2006 Conference of NAACL-HLT*, pages 49–52. Association for Computational Linguistics.

José Luis Iturrioz Leza and Paula López Gómez. 2006. *Gramática wixarika*, volume 1. Lincom Europa.

Katharina Kann, Manuel Mager, Ivan Meza, and Hinrich Shütze. 2018. Fortification of neural morphological segmentation models for polysynthetic minimal-resource languages. In *Proceedings of the 2018 Conference of the NAACL-HLT 2018*. North American chapter of the Association for Computational Linguistics.

Philipp Koehn and Hieu Hoang. 2007. Factored translation models. In *Proceedings of the 2007 joint conference EMNLP-CoNLL*.

Philipp Koehn. 2005. Europarl: A parallel corpus for statistical machine translation. In *MT summit*, volume 5, pages 79–86.

Yolanda Lastra de Suárez. 1980. Náhuatl de Acaxochitlán, Hidalgo. In *Archivos de lenguas indígenas de México*, volume 10. El Colegio de México.

Jason Lee, Kyunghyun Cho, and Thomas Hofmann. 2016. Fully character-level neural machine translation without explicit segmentation. *arXiv preprint arXiv:1610.03017*.

Jeff MacSwan. 1998. The argument status of nps in southeast puebla nahuatl: comments on the polysynthesis parameter. *Southwest Journal of Linguistics*, 17(2):101–114.

Manuel Mager and Ivan Meza. 2018. Hacia la traducción automática de las lenguas indígenas de méxico. In *Proceedings of the DH 2018*. The Association of Digital Humanities Organizations.

Jesús Manuel Mager Hois, Carlos Barrón Romero, and Ivan Vladimir Meza Ruiz. 2016. Traductor estadístico wixarika-español usando descomposición morfológica. In *Proceedings of COMTEL*. Universidad Inca Garcilaso de la Vega.

Jesus Manuel Mager Hois. 2017. Traductor híbrido wixárika - español con escasos recursos bilingües. Master's thesis, Universidad Autónoma Metropolitana.

Marianne Mithun. 1986. On the nature of noun incorporation. *Language*, 62(1):32–37.

J Ohanna Nichols. 1986. Head-marking and dependent-marking grammar. *Language*, 62(1):56–119.

Franz Josef Och and Hermann Ney. 2003. A systematic comparison of various statistical alignment models. *Computational Linguistics*, 29(1):19–51.

Kemal Oflazer. 2008. Statistical machine translation into a morphologically complex language. In *Proceeding of CICLing*, pages 376–387. Springer.

Peyman Passban, Qun Liu, and Andy Way. 2018. Improving character-based decoding using target-side morphological information for neural machine translation. In *Proceedings of the 2018 Conference of the NAACL-HLT*, volume 1, pages 58–68.

Passban Peyman, Way Andy, and Liu Qun. 2018. Tailoring neural architectures for translating from morphologically rich languages. In *Proceedings of the 2018 COLING)*. nternational Committee on Computational Linguistics.

Rico Sennrich, Barry Haddow, and Alexandra Birch. 2016. Neural machine translation of rare words with subword units. In *Proceedings of the 2016 Annual Meeting of the ACL*, volume 1, pages 1715–1725.

Sara Stymne. 2011. Pre-and postprocessing for statistical machine translation into germanic languages. In *Proceedings of the ACL 2011 Student Session*, pages 12–17. Association for Computational Linguistics.

Clara Vania and Adam Lopez. 2017. From characters to words to in between: Do we capture morphology? In *Proceedings of the 2017 Annual Meeting of the ACL*, pages 2016–2027. Association for Computational Linguistics.

Sami Virpioja, Jaakko J Väyrynen, Mathias Creutz, and Markus Sadeniemi. 2007. Morphology-aware statistical machine translation based on morphs induced in an unsupervised manner. *MT Summit XI*, 2007:491–498.

Sami Virpioja, Peter Smit, Stig-Arne Grönroos, Mikko Kurimo, et al. 2013. Morfessor 2.0: Python implementation and extensions for morfessor baseline.

Automatic Glossing in a Low-Resource Setting for Language Documentation

Sarah Moeller and **Mans Hulden**
Department of Linguistics
University of Colorado
`first.last@colorado.edu`

Abstract

Morphological analysis of morphologically rich and low-resource languages is important to both descriptive linguistics and natural language processing. Field efforts usually procure analyzed data in cooperation with native speakers who are capable of providing some level of linguistic information. Manually annotating such data is very expensive and the traditional process is arguably too slow in the face of language endangerment and loss. We report on a case study of learning to automatically gloss a Nakh-Daghestanian language, *Lezgi*, from a very small amount of seed data. We compare a conditional random field based sequence labeler and a neural encoder-decoder model and show that a nearly 0.9 F_1-score on labeled accuracy of morphemes can be achieved with 3,000 words of transcribed oral text. Errors are mostly limited to morphemes with high allomorphy. These results are potentially useful for developing rapid annotation and fieldwork tools to support documentation of other morphologically rich, endangered languages.

1 Introduction

Thousands of languages lack documented data necessary to describe them accurately. In the early 1990s it was suggested that linguistics might be the first academic discipline to preside over the its own demise, since numbers indicated that as much as 90% of the world's languages would be extinct by the end of the 21st century (Krauss, 1992). Linguists quickly responded by developing methodology to record previously under- or undocumented languages (Himmelmann, 1998). Almost as quickly, they realized that unannotated data of a language that is no longer spoken is almost as inaccessible as an undocumented language. Language documentation and the initial descriptive work that often accompanies it is time- and labor-intensive work, but it is foundational to the study of new languages. It also benefits the community of speakers by supporting efforts to revitalize or maintain the language. Although the estimated number of languages in imminent danger of extinction has been reduced (Simons and Lewis, 2013), the task remains urgent.

Computational linguistics generally considers human annotation prohibitively expensive because it relies on linguistic expertise (Buys and Botha, 2016). However, employing this expertise has long been accepted practice in documentary and descriptive linguistics. Documentation data is not produced by a linguist alone; rather, it is created in close cooperation with native speakers who receive minimal training in general linguistics and software. The documentation work includes transcription of oral recordings, translation, then ends with, as descriptive work begins with, interlinearization (i.e. POS-tagging, morpheme segmentation, and glossing). The first task alone may takes an average of 39 times longer than the original recording, according to a recent survey of field linguists (CoEDL, 2017). No matter how many oral texts are recorded during a field project, time constraints often mean that only the annotations required to support a particular short-term goal are completed. For example, the data used in the current paper was collected by a linguist for his MA thesis. Since his topic was verbs, only the verbs were thoroughly annotated. More funds had to be found to hire another native speaker who could simultaneously

Proceedings of Workshop on Polysynthetic Languages, pages 84–93
Santa Fe, New Mexico, USA, August 20-26, 2018.

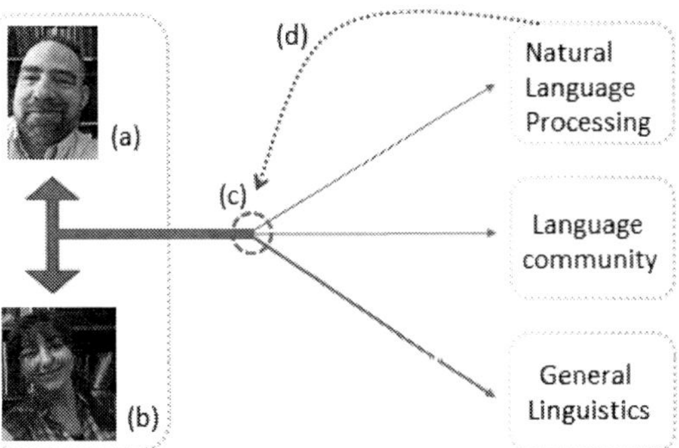

Figure 1: Flowchart of language data production. Descriptive linguists (a) collaborate with native speakers of a language (b) to produce documentary data for all subfields of linguistics, language development efforts by the community of speakers, and the extension of NLP tools to low-resource languages. A bottleneck of time-consuming annotation (c) keeps much of the data inaccessible to all but the community of speakers. The models described in this paper (d) attempt to employ semi-automated interlinearization to increase the trickle of data by .

learn and do basic linguistic analysis. Such manual work is slow and inevitably produces inconsistent annotations. It is noteworthy that many mistakes are not due to the difficulty of the task but because of its repetitive nature. In case marking languages, for example, morphemes marking subjects will be found in practically every clause and those marking objects, dative, or genitive arguments may be nearly as frequent. Only a small percentage of tokens contain unusual and interesting morphological forms. Thus, a large chunk of this highly time-consuming work is as monotonous to the annotator as it is uninformative to language science—in short, we are faced with a bottleneck (Holton et al., 2017; Simons, 2013).

After nearly 30 years of emphasis on increasing accessible documentation data, very few computational tools have been applied to this bottleneck. The most popular software packages designed for linguistic analysis, ELAN (Auer et al., 2010) and FLEx (Rogers, 2010), provide almost no automated aid for common, repetitive tasks, although FLEx does copy the annotator's work onto subsequent tokens if they are identical to previously analyzed tokens.

To address this problem, we apply machine learning models to two common tasks applied to documentation data: morpheme segmentation and glossing. The models use about 3,000 words of manually-annotated data that train sequence models to predict morpheme labels (and glosses). The goal is to achieve accurate results on more data in less time. A case study on *Lezgi* [lez] explores three issues as a first step toward integrating the models into linguistic analysis software. First, can the linguist and native speaker expect machine learning techniques to successfully widen the data bottleneck after they have manually annotated a few transcribed texts? Second, could a sequence labeler achieve reasonable accuracy using features that are generalizable to most languages? If a feature-based tool could be applied to several languages without tweaking features in a language-specific fashion, it would be accessible even to native speakers without linguistic skills who wish to create structured language data. At the same time, if high accuracy is achieved an agglutinative language like *Lezgi*, then minimal feature-tweaking could make the model equally successful on more fusional languages. Lastly, what might the errors in the case study indicate for typologically different languages?

Section 2 reviews related work. Section 3 introduces the case study and Section 4 describes the models used. The results are compared and analyzed in Section 5. Implications and future work are discussed in Section 6, before the conclusion in Section 7.

2   Related Work

Computational linguistics boasts a long history of successful unsupervised morphology learning (Goldsmith, 2001; Creutz and Lagus, 2005; Monson et al., 2007). One feature that unsupervised models share is the requirement for large amounts of data. Ironically, languages with large amounts of data available likely already have published morphological descriptions and some interlinearized text, even though they may be considered low-resource languages. Under-documented languages rarely have sufficient data for a thorough morphological description. If unsupervised approaches were better known among documentary linguists, it might encourage them to archive more minimally-annotated data, which is a high-priority but rarely-met goal in language documentation.

For language documentation methods, more interesting approaches are those that augment small amounts of supervised data with unsupervised data. Supervised and semi-supervised learning generally requires less data to train and yields better results than unsupervised methods (Ahlberg et al., 2014; Ruokolainen et al., 2013; Cotterell et al., 2015; Kann et al., 2017). Several recent CoNLL papers (Cotterell et al., 2017) showed that very small amounts of annotated data could be augmented by exploiting either structured, labeled data, raw texts, or even artificial data. This assumes, however, that the data has already been processed in some way and made accessible. This paper looks at ongoing annotation and not generally accessible data.

This paper is most closely related to experiments on whether active learning could speed the time-consuming analysis of documentation data (Baldridge and Palmer, 2009; Palmer, 2009; Palmer et al., 2010). The experiments used field data processed with linguistic analysis software that are no longer supported. Our paper uses data from FLEx, currently one of the two most popular software modules for linguistic analysis. Earlier work has encountered complications because the analysis of certain morphemes has changed the middle of the project. This is normal—linguistic analysis, especially when a language has not been well-described before, is a dynamic, continually evolving process. Palmer et al. (2010) performed unsupervised morphological processing and semi-automatic POS tagging, combined with active learning. This seems to assume that the data is transcribed but not annotated in any way and would be most appropriate near the beginning of a documentation project. By contrast, we use supervised learning methods on data already tagged for parts of speech and assume that the annotation process is well underway. We also assume a fixed morpheme analysis applied consistently to the data which makes the methods more appropriate for later stages of a documentation project, or for a project that is willing to start with an less-than-accurate analysis and make bulk changes in FLEx. Most generally, previous work in the field has examined several factors affecting speed and accuracy of the annotators and the results seem to demonstrate that machine-supported annotation holds great promise for speeding language documentation. That promise lays the foundation for our case study.

3   Case Study: Lezgi

Three sequence labelers were tested on transcribed oral data from the Qusar dialect of *Lezgi* [lez]. *Lezgi* belongs to the Nakh-Daghestanian (Northeast Caucasian) family. It is spoken by over 600,000 speakers in Russia and Azerbaijan (Simons and Fennig, 2017). The endangered Qusar dialect in Azerbaijan differs from the standard written dialect in several ways, including a locative case morpheme borrowed from Azerbaijani that is used alongside the native inessive (locative) case morpheme with the same meaning. The dialect also has freer word order. *Lezgi* is an highly agglutinative language with overwhelmingly suffixing morphology. Fourteen noun cases are built by case-stacking, a characteristic of Nakh-Daghestanian languages. Case-stacking is characterized by composing a case inflection by a sequence of morphemes instead of a unique morpheme for each case. A simplified example of Lezgi case-stacking is shown in Table 1. Case-stacking morpheme sequences can be de-constructed into individual agglutinating morphemes, or, since the semantics of the morphemes are not entirely compositional, the sequence can be viewed as a single, fusional morpheme. Verbal inflectional morphology is no less complicated, with 22 base affirmative forms, corresponding negative forms, and an often suppletive imperative stem. From these finite forms, affirmative and negative participles are formed, as well as secondary verb forms that communicate adverbial meanings or non-indicative moods.

The aim of this case study is to assist and speed human annotation of the documentation data. Our original goal was to perform segmentation and glossing with at least 80% accuracy. This goal is inspired by the Pareto Principle—the idea that 20% of one's effort produces 80% of one's results, and *vice*

itim-di	SG.ERG 'the man'	itim-ar	ABS-PL 'men'
itim-di-q	SG.POSTESSIVE 'behind the man'	itim-di-q-di	SG.POSTDIRECTIVE 'to behind the man'
itim-ar-di-k	PL-ADESSIVE 'at the men'	itim-ar-di-k-ay	PL-ADELATIVE 'from the men'

Table 1: An example of case-stacking on the Lezgi noun *itim* 'man'. Absolutive (ABS) case and singular number (SG) are unmarked. The plural suffix (PL) attaches directly to the noun stem. The ergative suffix (ERG) attaches in the second slot after the stem. Other cases add suffixes to the ergative morpheme (oblique stem (OBL) cf. Haspelmath (1993, p.74). The elative and directive meanings are added to the fourth slot after the stem. The semantics are only partially compositional. In the largest possible sequence (postdirective and adelative), the final (directive) *-di* and (elative) *ay* suffixes add directed-motion meaning to the penultimate locative (-essive) morphemes *k* or *q*, but the previous (ergative) morpheme seems to serve a purely grammatical purpose.

11.1
Word	Заз		дуьз	кичӀе	хьана	
Morphemes	за	-з	дуьз	кичӀе	хьа	-на
Lex. Gloss	1sg-ERG	DAT	great	fear	happened	AOR
Word Cat.	pro		adv	n	v	

Free I was so scared.

11.2
Word	За	лагьана		я	Аллагь		им	вуч	ятӀа	?
Morphemes	за	лагьа	-на	я	Аллагь		им	вуч	я	-тӀа
Lex. Gloss	1sg-ERG	say	AOR	oh	Allah		this	what	is	COND
Word Cat.	pro	v		prt	nprop		pro	interrog	v	

Free I asked: Oh God, what could it be?

Figure 2: Interlinearization in FLEx. Lezgi uses the Cyrillic alphabet. Segmentations are on the second line; glosses on the third. POS tags are below the glosses. The work is almost completely manual in FLEx. The goal is to complete the 2nd and 3rd lines automatically.

versa. A baseline that segmented correctly but assigned morphemes the majority label would perform at approximately 65% accuracy.

Data Ten texts amounting to a little over 3,000 words were excerpted from a small corpus of transcribed oral narratives. Of the 3,000 words, only nominals, pronouns, and verbs were morphologically analyzed. Every word had been tagged for part of speech. A linguist had provided morpheme glosses for all verbs. Other parts of speech were only partially glossed or segmented, if at all. A native speaker of the dialect finished segmenting the morphemes and glossed all affixes. The annotator often skipped core arguments with simple morphology, such as subjects or the extremely common aorist verbs, perhaps because the forms were so repetitive. She was more likely to annotate morphologically complex, but less common, tokens. Her initial annotations varied a great deal in quality, but once she identified morpheme boundaries, it was possible to refer to the descriptive grammar (Haspelmath, 1993) and make the annotations consistent. It seemed reasonable to expect that a native speaker educated in another language could quickly learn to recognize basic parts of speech in her own language, so the models assume that POS tags will exist in documentation data. The *Lezgi* data included two exceptions that are not basic parts of speech. Participles and demonstrative pronouns are more abstract than the general category of pronouns and verbs but these distinctions were kept simply because they had already been consistently annotated. After the linguist, native speaker, and author(s) each reviewed the gold standard annotations, all but three inflectional affixes had been accurately identified. These three were labeled UNK.

In our work, all but the neural model assume that (1) the data has been analyzed in FLEx, as shown in Figure 2, and exported as a FlexText XML format, (2) words have been tagged for part of speech, (for the case study - verb, participle, adjective, adverb, noun/proper noun, particle, pronoun, demonstrative pronoun, and postposition), (3) morpheme segmentation and glosses are consistent, and (4) all affixes, but not stems, are glossed. Inflectional morphemes are a closed class so the models could be easily trained to gloss them (e.g. ERG = ergative case, PST = past tense, etc.). Stems, however, are an open class, so the models were trained merely to recognize them as "stems". All characters that are not part

```
<morphemes>
  <morph type="stem" guid="d7f713e8-e8cf-11d3-9764-00c04f186933">
    <item type="txt" lang="lez-Cyrl-AZ-x-qusar">
      аял
    <item type="gls" lang="en">
  <morph type="suffix" guid="d7f713dd-e8cf-11d3-9764-00c04f186933">
    <item type="txt" lang="lez-Cyrl-AZ-x-qusar">
      -ар
    <item type="gls" lang="en">
      PL
<item type="pos" lang="en">
  n
```

Figure 3: Excerpt from FLExText XML format. It shows the morpheme breaks of one word consisting of a root morpheme followed by a plural suffix. The POS tag is attached at the word level.

of a word (e.g. digits and punctuation) were eliminated in pre-processing.

Pre-processing the data showed that even the most careful annotation team will make mistakes, even on a corpus as small as 3,000 words. A few POS tags and affix glosses were still missing, and others were incorrectly labeled. Non-linguist annotators may use slightly different labels for the same morpheme. As long as the computational linguist has expert knowledge of the language, missing glosses can be corrected as a debugging step. For incorrect labels, printing out tags allowed a linguist to spot check annotations and check if, for example, the distribution of POS tags appeared unusual.

Features Most of the extracted features generalize to all languages. Certain features, such as the number of surrounding letters viewed, are specific to *Lezgi*. Affixes in the language are rarely more than 3 letters long, so the models viewed only the surrounding 1–4 letters to ensure that at least one letter in the immediately surrounding morphemes was seen. However, the average length of a morpheme can be automatically calculated from the training data for any language. The features include an assumption that a unit labeled as "phrase" in FLEx is equivalent to a complete clause in the language. In reality, some "phrases" contain more than one sentence, some contain only a sentence fragment. This makes the word position feature inaccurate. The word position feature is the only feature customized to *Lezgi*. It is measured from the end of the phrase to take into account the language's strong tendency for verb-final word order. Other features, included position of the letter in the word, and, of course, POS tags taken from the data.

4 Model Description

This section describes three models that perform supervised morphological segmentation and labeling on limited data. All three models expect 2,000–3,000 words of cleanly annotated data. The first two expect the data to be annotated with POS tags.

4.1 Conditional Random Field

We use a linear-chain Conditional Random Field (CRF) (Lafferty et al., 2001) to train a sequence model where the input consists of individual characters and the output of a BIO-labeling (Ramshaw and Marcus, 1999) of the sequence, i.e. we treat this as a labeling problem of converting an input sequence of letters $\mathbf{x} = (x_1, \ldots, x_n)$ to an output sequence of BIO-labels $\mathbf{y} = (y_1, \ldots, y_n)$.

BIO-labeling In the training data, each letter is associated with a Beginning-Inside-Outside (BIO) tag—a type of tagging where each position is declared either the beginning (B) of a chunk or morpheme, inside (I) or outside (O). The BIO tags are specific to each type of morpheme. BIO tags include (1) the morpheme type for stem morphemes (e.g. B-stem) or (2) affix glosses (e.g. I-DAT for a non-initial letter of a morpheme marking dative case). This combination of BIO tags and specific labels allows the system to perform segmentation and labeling/glossing simultaneously. For example, in tagging the word ава, with the morphemes й (PTP), and ди (SBST) the representation would be as follows:

а	в	а	й	д	и	**input**
B-stem	I-stem	I-stem	B-PTP	B-SBST	I-SBST	**output**

CRF model   We model the conditional distribution of the output BIO-sequence $\mathbf{y}$, given the input $\mathbf{x}$ in the usual way as

$$p(\mathbf{y}|\mathbf{x}) = \frac{1}{Z}\exp\Big(\sum_{i=1}^{n}\phi(y_{i-1}, y_i, \mathbf{x}, i)\Big) \tag{1}$$

where ϕ is our feature extraction function which can be expressed through a sum of k individual component functions

$$\phi(y_{i-1}, y_i, \mathbf{x}, i) = \sum_{k} w_k f_k(y_{i-1}, y_i, \mathbf{x}, i) \tag{2}$$

Here, Z is the "partition function" which normalizes the expression to a proper distribution over all possible taggings given an input. We use the *CRFsuite* (Okazaki, 2007) implementation together with a Python API.[1]

The training parameters used L-BFGS optimization (Liu and Nocedal, 1989) and Elastic Net regularization, i.e. a linear combination of L_1 and L_2 penalties. Maximum iterations for early stopping were set at 50.

4.2   Segmentation and Labeling Pipeline: CRF+SVM

Since the subtask of morpheme segmentation is presumably much easier than joint segmentation and labeling, we also experimented with a pipeline model that would first segment and then label, where we could use a richer set of contextual features for the subsequent labeling process. Here, the CRF is employed only for segmentation and is used as described above but without the morpheme specific labels. After predicting BIO tags at the character-level, characters are combined into predicted morpheme strings. We then train a multi-class linear Support Vector Machine (SVM)[2] which classifies the segmented morphemes with the specific labels ("stem" or individual affix glosses). This allows the SVM to use surrounding morphemes as features (though not future labels). The SVM is trained on the concatenated features of every letter in each predicted morpheme but only the morpheme labels of the predicted initial letter.

4.3   Neural Model

As the currently strongest performing models for the related task of morphological inflection (Cotterell et al., 2017; Kann et al., 2017; Makarov et al., 2017) use an LSTM-based sequence-to-sequence (seq2seq) models (Sutskever et al., 2014) with an additional attention mechanism (Bahdanau et al., 2015), we also experiment with such a model for our task. In other words, we treat this as a translation task of input character sequences directly to output BIO-labels, as in the CRF model, but without POS-tags in the input. After initial experiments, we set the hidden layer size at 128, the batch size as 32, the *teacher forcing* (Williams and Zipser, 1989) ratio at 0.5. Similar to the CRF-model, it jointly predicts morpheme boundaries and specific BIO-labels.

5   Results

Once the features are extracted and the training complete, the models predict morpheme segmentation and morpheme type for stems, or glosses for affixes. This section discusses the results, compared in Table 2, of all three models. The goal was for a model to complete at least 80% of the segmentation and glossing correctly, leaving the most difficult, rare, and hopefully informative forms for a human to annotate. Originally, a 90/10 split was tried but the test data was encountering a dozen or less labels. With an 80/20 split, the test encountered nearly twice as many labels and the variance of F_1-score was less between each test run. All three models performed near or above the target.

Joint segmentation and glossing/labeling produced the best results. The data is read letter by letter and each letter is associated with a BIO tag and specific morpheme type/gloss label. This identifies the letters

---

[1] https://python-crfsuite.readthedocs.io/en/latest/
[2] Using the LIBLINEAR implementation (Fan et al., 2008).

CRF	pipeline	seq2seq
0.895	0.861	0.763

Table 2: Labeled position results (F_1-score) compared across CRF-only, CRF+SVM pipeline, and seq2seq models. The first two are averages across multiple runs on random data splits.

in the morphemes as well as the morpheme boundaries. The letters were grouped into predicted morphemes for labeled position evaluation. Table 3 demonstrates the model's ability to produce reasonable results with limited training data. It appears that for *Lezgi* 3,000 words is a sufficient number of training examples.

Label	Precision	Recall	F_1	Instances
stem	0.98	0.97	0.97	127
AOR	0.93	1.00	0.97	14
FOC	1.00	1.00	1.00	10
OBL	0.75	0.67	0.71	9
GEN	0.67	0.40	0.50	5
ERG	0.67	0.40	0.50	5
DAT	1.00	1.00	1.00	4
NEG	1.00	0.75	0.86	4
PTP	0.80	1.00	0.89	4
SBST	1.00	1.00	1.00	3
IMPF	1.00	1.00	1.00	2
PERF	1.00	1.00	1.00	2
ELAT	1.00	1.00	1.00	1
SUPER	1.00	1.00	1.00	1
total/avg all	0.92	0.87	0.90	191
total/avg affixes	0.84	0.80	0.82	64

Table 3: CRF-only model labeled position results from one run over a randomized test set with 80/20 split. Averages are macroaverages.

The most acute issue is the reduction of accuracy when predicting stems compared to predicting affixes. The last line of Table 3 shows that the precision, recall, and F_1-scores of affixes have lower performance compared with the overall scores. The pipeline model results discussed in below results in a similar pattern but slightly worse results. Since training was done at character-level and affixes tend to be 1–3 letters long while stem length varies greatly, transitions between morphemes become less accurate. Also, single-letter affixes may coincide with any first or last letter of possible surrounding morphemes. The classifier is, however, adept at splitting affixes from stems, and this in itself would be helpful to human annotators. The good results on the much larger number of stems suggests that the performance on affixes will keep improving as training examples increase.

The model was provided with no information about the language's morphophonology. Its accuracy strongly correlates with the extent of isomorphism between affixes or the amount of allomorphy that a particular affix exhibits. Most affixes are unique from other morphemes and have few or no variant forms. On the other hand, the oblique affix and the ergative case morpheme are identical, but the ergative morpheme is always the last morpheme on a word while the oblique is always followed by other case morphemes. Letter position features should have caught this difference. However, the oblique and ergative case also have more allomorphs (over 10 different forms) than any other morpheme. The genitive case and the aorist tense morphemes are identical to some other morphemes, which also causes difficulty. All but a handful of affixes are identified with very high accuracy. These exceptions—aorist tense (AOR) - identical to the aorist converb, genitive case (GEN) - identical to the nominalized verb marker (masdar), ergative case (ERG) and the oblique affix (OBL) which are identical to each other and highly allomorphic—indicate that limited data may not be sufficient for languages with extensive allomorphy.

When the CRF is placed in a pipeline with a SVM classifier, the CRF only identified morpheme boundaries. Overall accuracy of the pipeline was worse than the CRF-only model, achieving an average 0.86 F_1-score. This echoes the findings of Cohen and Smith (2007) and Lee et al. (2011) that joint training of syntax and morphology produce better results than separate training. The pipeline model had slightly higher accuracy on morphemes with multiple allomorphs but tended to perform worse on less frequent morphemes.

Lastly, the data was run on a bidirectional sequence-to-sequence deep neural network. The best result on the test set was over 0.76 F_1, reached at 500 epochs with early stopping.

6 Discussion and Future Work

It is crucial to test the models on other languages, especially polysynthetic languages which may not have many more morphemes per word but have more fusion and may have more complicated morphophonology. Requests were sent to field linguists working in a variety of languages, but time constraints did not allow them to achieve consistent annotation on a sufficient number of words. Yet, most features described in Section 3 are basic for all languages. It seems reasonable that extracting features specific to polysynthetic languages could produce just as high results.

The feature-based models surpassed the 80% accuracy goal using features informed by general linguistic knowledge or features that can be extracted directly from data. These features proved sufficient for *Lezgi*, though expanding to other languages might uncover other general linguistic features that would maintain high accuracy for more languages. If generic features prove insufficient, questions could be presented to linguists who provide the data and language-specific features could be extracted based on their input. The questionnaire of the LinGO Grammar Matrix (Bender et al., 2002) is a possible initial model for an interface.

The poorer results caused by the language's allomorphy do not bode well for languages with more complex series of allomorphs. An interactive interface could request human annotators for infrequent or problematic inflected forms, or such cases where the model has little confidence in the labeling. For example, noun stems harvested from FLEx's automatic lexicon builder could be presented for a *Lezgi* annotator to provide the various ergative and oblique morphemes. These single forms would augment annotated text.

Predicted morphemes and glosses need to be checked and corrected by trained annotators. Previous experiments (Baldridge and Palmer, 2009; Palmer, 2009; Palmer et al., 2010) strongly imply that vetting a portion of the data and correcting a smaller portion of machine-generated annotations is faster than manually annotating every single token. The next step is to bring the human back into the training loop by having the native speaker check and correct the model's performance on unlabeled data. The corrections would serve as additional supervised data. As more texts are annotated with the help of the model, more data could be fed into the training, increasing accuracy. In addition, although currently only affixes are glossed, the model could leverage its high success at identifying stems and present them to be glossed so that they could be added to future training data. Each iteration of prediction and correction will incrementally speed the task. In the future, it is hoped that automated support for annotation could be integrated with software such as FLEx, or another interface familiar to documentary and descriptive linguists.

7 Conclusion

We have explored a case study on *Lezgi* to examine whether machine learning techniques could break the bottleneck of documentation data production by achieving reasonable accuracy using a few interlinearized texts and general linguistic features. The results demonstrate that current NLP tools and human and data resources commonly found in documentary linguistic field projects can be combined in order to speed annotation of valuable documentary data. A CRF classifier, a CRF+SVM pipeline, and a neural seq2seq model were tested and compared to show that machine learning could remove up to 90% of that labor from human annotators and place it upon a potential field assistant tool. Models such as these could be integrated into the workflow of language documentation and force open the annotation bottleneck. Further training should improve the accuracy of the model which, in turn, will further speed the availability of new language data. This will increase the amount of natural language data available to the language communities, linguists, and computational experiments. It achieves high accuracy with basic cross-linguistic features. A little feature engineering might transfer the high success to polysynthetic and fusional languages, or at least achieve the original Pareto tradeoff goal of 80%.[3]

References

Malin Ahlberg, Markus Forsberg, and Mans Hulden. 2014. Semi-supervised learning of morphological paradigms and lexicons. In *Proceedings of the 14th Conference of the European Chapter of the Association for Computational Linguistics*, pages 569–578. Association for Computational Linguistics.

Eric Auer, Albert Russel, Han Sloetjes, Peter Wittenburg, Oliver Schreer, S. Masnieri, Daniel Schneider, and Sebastian Tschöpel. 2010. ELAN as flexible annotation framework for sound and image processing detectors. In Nicoletta Calzolari, Khalid Choukri, Bente Maegaard, Joseph Mariani, Jan Odijk, Stelios Piperidis, Mike Rosner, and Daniel Tapias, editors, *European Language Resources Association LREC 2010: Proceedings of the 7th International Language Resources and Evaluation*, pages 890–893. European Language Resources Association.

Dzmitry Bahdanau, Kyunghyun Cho, and Yoshua Bengio. 2015. Neural machine translation by jointly learning to align and translate. In *ICLR*.

Jason Baldridge and Alexis Palmer. 2009. How well does active learning actually work? Time-based evaluation of cost-reduction strategies for language documentation. In *Proceedings of the 2009 Conference on Empirical Methods in Natural Language Processing*, pages 296–305. Association for Computational Linguistics.

Emily M. Bender, Dan Flickinger, and Stephan Oepen. 2002. The Grammar Matrix: An open-source starter-kit for the rapid development of cross-linguistically consistent broad-coverage precision grammars. In *Proceedings of the 2002 workshop on Grammar engineering and evaluation—Volume 15*, pages 1–7. Association for Computational Linguistics.

Jan Buys and Jan A. Botha. 2016. Cross-lingual morphological tagging for low-resource languages. In *Proceedings of the 54th Annual Meeting of the Association for Computational Linguistics (Volume 1: Long Papers)*, pages 1954–1964.

CoEDL. 2017. Early results from survey exploring transcription processes. `http://www.dynamicsoflanguage.edu.au/news-and-media/latest-headlines/article/?id=early-results-from-survey-exploring-transcription-processes`. Accessed: 2018-06-26.

Shay B. Cohen and Noah A. Smith. 2007. Joint morphological and syntactic disambiguation. In *Proceedings of the 2007 Joint Conference on Empirical Methods in Natural Language Processing and Computational Natural Language Learning*, pages 208–217. Association for Computational Linguistics.

Ryan Cotterell, Thomas Müller, Alexander M. Fraser, and Hinrich Schütze. 2015. Labeled morphological segmentation with semi-markov models. In *CoNLL-SIGMORPHON 2017 Shared Task: Universal Morphological Reinflection in 52 Languages*, pages 164–174.

Ryan Cotterell, Christo Kirov, John Sylak-Glassman, Gèraldine Walther, Ekaterina Vylomova, Patrick Xia, Manaal Faruqui, Sandra Kübler, David Yarowsky, Jason Eisner, and Mans Hulden. 2017. CoNLL-SIGMORPHON 2017 shared task: Universal morphological reinflection in 52 languages. In *CoNLL*, pages 1–30. Association for Computational Linguistics.

Mathias Creutz and Krista Lagus. 2005. *Unsupervised morpheme segmentation and morphology induction from text corpora using Morfessor 1.0*. Helsinki University of Technology Helsinki.

Rong-En Fan, Kai-Wei Chang, Cho-Jui Hsieh, Xiang-Rui Wang, and Chih-Jen Lin. 2008. LIBLINEAR: A library for large linear classification. *Journal of machine learning research*, 9(Aug):1871–1874.

[3]We gratefully acknowledge the support of NVIDIA Corporation with the donation of the Titan Xp GPU used for this research.

John Goldsmith. 2001. Unsupervised learning of the morphology of a natural language. *Computational linguistics*, 27(2):153–198.

Martin Haspelmath. 1993. *A grammar of Lezgian*. Walter de Gruyter, Berlin.

Nikolaus P. Himmelmann. 1998. Documentary and descriptive linguistics. *Linguistics*, 36(1):161–196.

Gary Holton, Kavon Hooshiar, and Nicholas Thieberger. 2017. Developing collection management tools to create more robust and reliable linguistic data. In *Workshop on Computational Methods for Endangered Languages*.

Katharina Kann, Ryan Cotterell, and Hinrich Schütze. 2017. Neural multi-source morphological reinflection. In *Proceedings of the 15th Conference of the European Chapter of the Association for Computational Linguistics: Volume 1, Long Papers*, pages 514–524. Association for Computational Linguistics.

Michael Krauss. 1992. The world's languages in crisis. *Language*, 68(1):4–10.

John Lafferty, Andrew McCallum, and Fernando C. N. Pereira. 2001. Conditional random fields: Probabilistic models for segmenting and labeling sequence data. In *Proceedings of the Eighteenth International Conference on Machine Learning*, pages 282–289.

Yoong Keok Lee, Aria Haghighi, and Regina Barzilay. 2011. Modeling syntactic context improves morphological segmentation. In *Proceedings of the Fifteenth Conference on Computational Natural Language Learning*, pages 1–9. Association for Computational Linguistics.

Dong C. Liu and Jorge Nocedal. 1989. On the limited memory BFGS method for large scale optimization. *Mathematical Programming*, 45(1-3):503–528.

Peter Makarov, Tatiana Ruzsics, and Simon Clematide. 2017. Align and copy: UZH at SIGMORPHON 2017 shared task for morphological reinflection. In *Proceedings of the CoNLL SIGMORPHON 2017 Shared Task: Universal Morphological Reinflection*, pages 49–57. Association for Computational Linguistics.

Christian Monson, Jaime Carbonell, Alon Lavie, and Lori Levin. 2007. ParaMor: Finding paradigms across morphology. In *Advances in Multilingual and Multimodal Information Retrieval*, Lecture Notes in Computer Science, pages 900–907. Springer, Berlin, Heidelberg.

Naoaki Okazaki. 2007. Crfsuite: a fast implementation of conditional random fields (CRFs). http://www.chokkan.org/software/crfsuite/.

Alexis Palmer, Taesun Moon, Jason Baldridge, Katrin Erk, Eric Campbell, and Telma Can. 2010. Computational strategies for reducing annotation effort in language documentation. *Linguistic Issues in Language Technology*, 3(4):1–42.

Alexis Mary Palmer. 2009. *Semi-automated annotation and active learning for language documentation*. Phd thesis, University of Texas at Austin.

Lance A. Ramshaw and Mitchell P. Marcus. 1999. Text chunking using transformation-based learning. In *Natural language processing using very large corpora*, pages 157–176. Springer.

Chris Rogers. 2010. Review of fieldworks language explorer (FLEx) 3.0. *Language Documentation & Conservation*, 04:78–84.

Teemu Ruokolainen, Oskar Kohonen, Sami Virpioja, and Mikko Kurimo. 2013. Supervised morphological segmentation in a low-resource learning setting using conditional random fields. In *CoNLL*, pages 29–37.

Gary F. Simons and Charles D. Fennig. 2017. Ethnologue. Languages of the world. *SIL, Dallas, Texas*.

Gary F. Simons and M. Paul Lewis. 2013. The world's languages in crisis. *Responses to language endangerment: In honor of Mickey Noonan. New directions in language documentation and language revitalization*, 3:20.

Gary F. Simons. 2013. Requirements for implementing the AARDVARC vision. Presented at workshop of the Automatically Annotated Repository of Digital Video and Audio Resources Community (AARDVARC), Eastern Michigan University, Ypsilanti, May 9-11, 2013.

Ilya Sutskever, Oriol Vinyals, and Quoc V. Le. 2014. Sequence to sequence learning with neural networks. In *Advances in Neural Information Processing Systems (NIPS)*, pages 3104–3112.

Ronald J. Williams and David Zipser. 1989. A learning algorithm for continually running fully recurrent neural networks. *Neural computation*, 1(2):270–280.

Author Index